IDLE IDEAS IN 1905

IDLE IDEAS IN 1905

JEROME K. JEROME

Serenity
Publishers, LLC
ROCKVILLE, MARYLAND
2009

ISBN: 978-1-60450-726-3

Published by Serenity Publishers
An Arc Manor Company
P. O. Box 10339
Rockville, MD 20849-0339
www.SerenityPublishers.com
Printed in the United States of America/United Kingdom

CONTENTS

ARE WE AS INTERESTING AS WE THINK WE ARE?

"*Charmed.* Very hot weather we've been having of late—I mean cold. Let me see, I did not quite catch your name just now. Thank you so much. Yes, it is a bit close." And a silence falls, neither of us being able to think what next to say.

What has happened is this: My host has met me in the doorway, and shaken me heartily by the hand.

"So glad you were able to come," he has said. "Some friends of mine here, very anxious to meet you." He has bustled me across the room. "Delightful people. You'll like them—have read all your books."

He has brought me up to a stately lady, and has presented me. We have exchanged the customary commonplaces, and she, I feel, is waiting for me to say something clever, original and tactful. And I don't know whether she is Presbyterian or Mormon; a Protectionist or a Free Trader; whether she is engaged to be married or has lately been divorced!

A friend of mine adopts the sensible plan of always providing you with a short history of the person to whom he is about to lead you.

"I want to introduce you to a Mrs. Jones," he whispers. "Clever woman. Wrote a book two years ago. Forget the name of it. Something about twins. Keep away from sausages. Father ran a pork shop in the Borough. Husband on the Stock Exchange. Keep off coke. Unpleasantness about a company. You'll get on best by sticking to the book. Lot in it about platonic friendship. Don't seem to be looking too closely at her. Has a slight squint she tries to hide."

By this time we have reached the lady, and he introduces me as a friend of his who is simply dying to know her.

"Wants to talk about your book," he explains. "Disagrees with you entirely on the subject of platonic friendship. Sure you'll be able to convince him."

It saves us both a deal of trouble. I start at once on platonic friendship, and ask her questions about twins, avoiding sausages and coke. She thinks me an unusually interesting man, and I am less bored than otherwise I might be.

I have sometimes thought it would be a serviceable device if, in Society, we all of us wore a neat card—pinned, say, upon our back— setting forth such information as was necessary; our name legibly written, and how to be pronounced; our age (not necessarily in good faith, but for purposes of conversation. Once I seriously hurt a German lady by demanding of her information about the Franco-German war. She looked to me as if she could not object to being taken for forty. It turned out she was thirty-seven. Had I not been an Englishman I might have had to fight a duel); our religious and political beliefs; together with a list of the subjects we were most at home upon; and a few facts concerning our career—sufficient to save the stranger from, what is vulgarly termed "putting his foot in it." Before making jokes about "Dumping," or discussing the question of Chinese Cheap Labour, one would glance behind and note whether one's companion was ticketed "Whole-hogger," or "Pro-Boer." Guests desirous of agreeable partners—an "agreeable person," according to the late Lord Beaconsfield's definition, being "a person who agrees with you"—could make their own selection.

"Excuse me. Would you mind turning round a minute? Ah, 'Wagnerian Crank!' I am afraid we should not get on together. I prefer the Italian school."

Or, "How delightful. I see you don't believe in vaccination. May I take you into supper?"

Those, on the other hand, fond of argument would choose a suitable opponent. A master of ceremonies might be provided who would stand in the centre of the room and call for partners: "Lady with strong views in favour of female franchise wishes to meet gentleman holding the opinions of St. Paul. With view to argument."

An American lady, a year or two ago, wrote me a letter that did me real good: she appreciated my work with so much understanding, criticised it with such sympathetic interest. She added that, when in England the summer before, she had been on the point of accepting an invitation to meet me; but at the last moment she had changed her mind; she felt so sure—she put it pleasantly, but this is what it came to—that in my own proper person I should fall short of her expectations. For my own sake I felt sorry she had cried off; it would have been worth something to have met so sensible a woman. An author introduced to people who have read—or who say that they have read—his books, feels always like a man taken for the first time to be shown to his future wife's relations. They are very pleasant. They try to put him at his ease. But he knows instinctively they are disappointed with him. I remember, when a very young man, attending a party at which a famous American humorist was the chief guest. I was standing close behind a lady who was talking to her husband.

"He doesn't look a bit funny," said the lady.

"Great Scott!" answered her husband. "How did you expect him to look? Did you think he would have a red nose and a patch over one eye?"

"Oh, well, he might look funnier than that, anyhow," retorted the lady, highly dissatisfied. "It isn't worth coming for."

We all know the story of the hostess who, leaning across the table during the dessert, requested of the funny man that he would kindly say something amusing soon, because the dear children were waiting to go to bed. Children, I suppose, have no use for funny people who don't choose to be funny. I once invited a friend down to my house for a Saturday to Monday. He is an entertaining man, and before he came I dilated on his powers of humour—somewhat foolishly perhaps— in the presence of a certain youthful person who resides with me, and who listens when she oughtn't to, and never when she ought. He happened not to be in a humorous mood that evening. My young relation, after dinner, climbed upon my knee. For quite five minutes she sat silent. Then she whispered:

"Has he said anything funny?"

"Hush. No, not yet; don't be silly."

Five minutes later: "Was that funny?"

"No, of course not."

"Why not?"

"Because—can't you hear? We are talking about Old Age Pensions."

"What's that?"

"Oh, it's—oh, never mind now. It isn't a subject on which one can be funny."

"Then what's he want to talk about it for?"

She waited for another quarter of an hour. Then, evidently bored, and much to my relief, suggested herself that she might as well go to bed. She ran to me the next morning in the garden with an air of triumph.

"He said something so funny last night," she told me.

"Oh, what was it?" I inquired. It seemed to me I must have missed it.

"Well, I can't exactly 'member it," she explained, "not just at the moment. But it was so funny. I dreamed it, you know."

For folks not Lions, but closely related to Lions, introductions must be trying ordeals. You tell them that for years you have been yearning to meet them. You assure them, in a voice trembling with emotion, that this is indeed a privilege. You go on to add that when a boy—

At this point they have to interrupt you to explain that they are not the Mr. So-and-So, but only his cousin or his grandfather; and all you can think of to say is: "Oh, I'm so sorry."

I had a nephew who was once the amateur long-distance bicycle champion. I have him still, but he is stouter and has come down to a motor car. In sporting circles I was always introduced as "Shorland's Uncle." Close-cropped young men would gaze at me with rapture; and then inquire: "And do you do anything yourself, Mr. Jerome?"

But my case was not so bad as that of a friend of mine, a doctor. He married a leading actress, and was known ever afterwards as "Miss B—'s husband."

At public dinners, where one takes one's seat for the evening next to someone that one possibly has never met before, and is never likely to meet again, conversation is difficult and dangerous. I remember talking to a lady at a Vagabond Club dinner. She asked me during the entree—with a light laugh, as I afterwards recalled—what I thought, candidly, of the last book of a certain celebrated authoress. I told her, and a coldness sprang up between us. She happened to be the certain celebrated authoress; she had changed her place at the last moment so as to avoid sitting next to another lady novelist, whom she hated.

One has to shift oneself, sometimes, on these occasions. A newspaper man came up to me last Ninth of November at the Mansion House.

"Would you mind changing seats with me?" he asked. "It's a bit awkward. They've put me next to my first wife."

I had a troubled evening myself once long ago. I accompanied a young widow lady to a musical At Home, given by a lady who had more acquaintances than she knew. We met the butler at the top of the stairs. My friend spoke first:

"Say Mrs. Dash and—"

The butler did not wait for more—he was a youngish man—but shouted out:

"Mr. and Mrs. Dash."

"My dear! how very quiet you have kept!" cried our hostess delighted. "Do let me congratulate you."

The crush was too great and our hostess too distracted at the moment for any explanations. We were swept away, and both of us spent the remainder of the evening feebly protesting our singleness.

If it had happened on the stage it would have taken us the whole play to get out of it. Stage people are not allowed to put things right when mistakes are made with their identity. If the light comedian is expecting a plumber, the first man that comes into the drawing-room has got to be a plumber. He is not allowed to point out that he never was a plumber; that he doesn't look like a plumber; that no one not an idiot would mistake him for a plumber. He has got to be shut up in the bathroom and have water poured over him, just as if he were a plumber—a stage plumber, that is. Not till right away at the end of the last act is he permitted to remark that he happens to be the new curate.

I sat out a play once at which most people laughed. It made me sad. A dear old lady entered towards the end of the first act. We knew she was the aunt. Nobody can possibly mistake the stage aunt—except the people on the stage. They, of course, mistook her for a circus rider, and shut her up in a cupboard. It is what cupboards seem to be reserved for on the stage. Nothing is ever put in them excepting the hero's relations. When she wasn't in the cupboard she was in a clothes basket, or tied up in a curtain. All she need have done was to hold on to something while remarking to the hero:

"If you'll stop shouting and jumping about for just ten seconds, and give me a chance to observe that I am your maiden aunt from Devonshire, all this tomfoolery can be avoided."

That would have ended it. As a matter of fact that did end it five minutes past eleven. It hadn't occurred to her to say it before.

In real life I never knew but of one case where a man suffered in silence unpleasantness he could have ended with a word; and that was the case of the late Corney Grain. He had been engaged to give his entertainment at a country house. The lady was a nouvelle riche of snobbish instincts. She left instructions that Corney Grain when he arrived was to dine with the servants. The butler, who knew better, apologised; but Corney was a man not easily disconcerted. He dined well, and after dinner rose and addressed the assembled company.

"Well, now, my good friends," said Corney, "if we have all finished, and if you are all agreeable, I shall be pleased to present to you my little show."

The servants cheered. The piano was dispensed with. Corney contrived to amuse his audience very well for half-an-hour without it. At ten o'clock came down a message: Would Mr. Corney Grain come up into the drawing-room. Corney went. The company in the drawing-room were waiting, seated.

"We are ready, Mr. Grain," remarked the hostess.

"Ready for what?" demanded Corney.

"For your entertainment," answered the hostess.

"But I have given it already," explained Corney; "and my engagement was for one performance only."

"Given it! Where? When?"

"An hour ago, downstairs."

"But this is nonsense," exclaimed the hostess.

"It seemed to me somewhat unusual," Corney replied; "but it has always been my privilege to dine with the company I am asked to entertain. I took it you had arranged a little treat for the servants."

And Corney left to catch his train.

Another entertainer told me the following story, although a joke against himself. He and Corney Grain were sharing a cottage on the river. A man called early one morning to discuss affairs, and was talking to Corney in the parlour, which was on the ground floor. The window was open. The other entertainer—the man who told me the story—was dressing in the room above. Thinking he recognised the voice of the visitor below, he leant out of his bedroom window to hear better. He leant too far, and dived head foremost into a bed of flowers, his bare legs—and only his bare legs—showing through the open window of the parlour.

"Good gracious!" exclaimed the visitor, turning at the moment and seeing a pair of wriggling legs above the window sill; "who's that?"

Corney fixed his eyeglass and strolled to the window.

"Oh, it's only What's-his-name," he explained. "Wonderful spirits. Can be funny in the morning."

SHOULD WOMEN BE BEAUTIFUL?

Pretty women are going to have a hard time of it later on. Hitherto, they have had things far too much their own way. In the future there are going to be no pretty girls, for the simple reason there will be no plain girls against which to contrast them. Of late I have done some systematic reading of ladies' papers. The plain girl submits to a course of "treatment." In eighteen months she bursts upon Society an acknowledged beauty. And it is all done by kindness. One girl writes:

"Only a little while ago I used to look at myself in the glass and cry. Now I look at myself and laugh."

The letter is accompanied by two photographs of the young lady. I should have cried myself had I seen her as she was at first. She was a stumpy, flat-headed, squat-nosed, cross-eyed thing. She did not even look good. One virtue she appears to have had, however. It was faith. She believed what the label said, she did what the label told her. She is now a tall, ravishing young person, her only trouble being, I should say, to know what to do with her hair—it reaches to her knees and must be a nuisance to her. She would do better to give some of it away. Taking this young lady as a text, it means that the girl who declines to be a dream of loveliness does so out of obstinacy. What the raw material may be does not appear to matter. Provided no feature is absolutely missing, the result is one and the same.

Arrived at years of discretion, the maiden proceeds to choose the style of beauty she prefers. Will she be a Juno, a Venus, or a Helen? Will she have a Grecian nose, or one tip-tilted like the petal of a rose? Let her try the tip-tilted style first. The professor has an idea it is going to be fashionable. If afterwards she does not like it, there will be time to try the Grecian. It is difficult to decide these points without experiment.

Would the lady like a high or a low forehead? Some ladies like to look intelligent. It is purely a matter of taste. With the Grecian nose, the low broad forehead perhaps goes better. It is more according to precedent. On the other hand, the high brainy forehead would be more original. It is for the lady herself to select.

We come to the question of eyes. The lady fancies a delicate blue, not too pronounced a colour—one of those useful shades that go with almost everything. At the same time there should be depth and passion. The professor understands exactly the sort of eye the lady means. But it will be expensive. There is a cheap quality; the professor does not recommend it. True that it passes muster by gaslight, but the sunlight shows it up. It lacks tenderness, and at the price you can hardly expect it to contain much hidden meaning. The professor advises the melting, Oh-George-take-me-in-your-arms-and-still-my-foolish-fears brand. It costs a little more, but it pays for itself in the end.

Perhaps it will be best, now the eye has been fixed upon, to discuss the question of the hair. The professor opens his book of patterns. Maybe the lady is of a wilful disposition. She loves to run laughing through the woods during exceptionally rainy weather; or to gallop across the downs without a hat, her fair ringlets streaming in the wind, the old family coachman panting and expostulating in the rear. If one may trust the popular novel, extremely satisfactory husbands have often been secured in this way. You naturally look at a girl who is walking through a wood, laughing heartily apparently for no other reason than because it is raining—who rides at stretch gallop without a hat. If you have nothing else to do, you follow her. It is always on the cards that such a girl may do something really amusing before she gets home. Thus things begin.

To a girl of this kind, naturally curly hair is essential. It must be the sort of hair that looks better when it is soaking wet. The bottle of stuff that makes this particular hair to grow may be considered dear, if you think merely of the price. But that is not the way to look at it. "What is it going to do for me?" That is what the girl has got to ask herself. It does not do to spoil the ship for a ha'porth of tar, as the saying is. If you are going to be a dashing, wilful beauty, you must have the hair for it, or the whole scheme falls to the ground.

Eyebrows and eyelashes, the professor assumes, the lady would like to match the hair. Too much eccentricity the professor does not agree with. Nature, after all, is the best guide; neatness combined with taste, that is the ideal to be aimed at. The eyebrows should be almost straight, the professor thinks; the eyelashes long and silky, with just the suspicion of a curl. The professor would also suggest a little less cheekbone. Cheekbones are being worn low this season.

Will the lady have a dimpled chin, or does she fancy the square-cut jaw? Maybe the square-cut jaw and the firm, sweet mouth are more suitable for the married woman. They go well enough with the baby and the tea-urn, and the strong, proud man in the background. For the unmarried girl the dimpled chin and the rosebud mouth are, perhaps, on the whole safer. Some gentlemen are so nervous of that firm, square jaw. For the present, at all events, let us keep to the rosebud and the dimple.

Complexion! Well, there is only one complexion worth considering—a creamy white, relieved by delicate peach pink. It goes with everything, and is always effective. Rich olives, striking pallors— yes, you hear of these things doing well. The professor's experience, however, is that for all-round work you will never improve upon the plain white and pink. It is less liable to get out of order, and is the easiest at all times to renew.

For the figure, the professor recommends something lithe and supple. Five foot four is a good height, but that is a point that should be discussed first with the dressmaker. For trains, five foot six is, perhaps, preferable. But for the sporting girl, who has to wear short frocks, that height would, of course, be impossible.

The bust and the waist are also points on which the dressmaker should be consulted. Nothing should be done in a hurry. What is the fashion going to be for the next two or three seasons? There are styles demanding that beginning at the neck you should curve out, like a pouter pigeon. There is apparently no difficulty whatever in obtaining this result. But if crinolines, for instance, are likely to come in again! The lady has only to imagine it for herself: the effect might be grotesque, suggestive of a walking hour-glass. So, too, with the waist. For some fashions it is better to have it just a foot from the neck. At other times it is more useful lower down. The lady will kindly think over these details and let the professor know. While one is about it, one may as well make a sound job.

It is all so simple, and, when you come to think of it, really not expensive. Age, apparently, makes no difference. A woman is as old as she looks. In future, I take it, there will be no ladies over five-and-twenty. Wrinkles! Why any lady should still persist in wearing them is a mystery to me. With a moderate amount of care any middle-class woman could save enough out of the housekeeping money in a month to get rid of every one of them. Grey hair! Well, of course, if you cling to grey hair, there is no more to be said. But to ladies who would just as soon have rich wavy-brown or a delicate shade of gold, I would point out that there are one hundred and forty-seven inexpensive lotions on the market, any one of which, rubbed gently into the head with a tooth-brush (not too hard) just before going to bed will, to use a colloquialism, do the trick.

Are you too stout, or are you too thin? All you have to do is to say which, and enclose stamps. But do not make a mistake and send for the wrong recipe. If you are already too thin, you might in consequence suddenly disappear before you found out your mistake. One very stout lady I knew worked at herself for eighteen months and got stouter every day. This discouraged her so much that she gave up trying. No doubt she had made a muddle and had sent for the wrong bottle, but she would not listen to further advice. She said she was tired of the whole thing.

In future years there will be no need for a young man to look about him for a wife; he will take the nearest girl, tell her his ideal, and, if she really care for him, she will go to the shop and have herself fixed up to his pattern. In certain Eastern countries, I believe, something of this kind is done. A gentleman desirous of adding to his family sends round the neighbourhood the weight and size of his favourite wife, hinting that if another can be found of the same proportions, there is room for her. Fathers walk round among their daughters, choose the most likely specimen, and have her fattened up. That is their brutal Eastern way. Out West we shall be more delicate. Match-making mothers will probably revive the old confession book. Eligible bachelors will be invited to fill in a page: "Your favourite height in women," "Your favourite measurement round the waist," "Do you like brunettes or blondes?"

The choice will be left to the girls.

"I do think Henry William just too sweet for words," the maiden of the future will murmur to herself. Gently, coyly, she will draw from him his ideal of what a woman should be. In from six months to a year she will burst upon him, the perfect She; height, size, weight, right to a T. He will clasp her in his arms.

"At last," he will cry, "I have found her, the woman of my dreams."

And if he does not change his mind, and the bottles do not begin to lose their effect, there will be every chance that they will be happy ever afterwards.

Might not Science go even further? Why rest satisfied with making a world of merely beautiful women? Cannot Science, while she is about it, make them all good at the same time. I do not apologise for the suggestion. I used to think all women beautiful and good. It is their own papers that have disillusioned me. I used to look at this lady or at that—shyly, when nobody seemed to be noticing me—and think how fair she was, how stately. Now I only wonder who is her chemist.

They used to tell me, when I was a little boy, that girls were made of sugar and spice. I know better now. I have read the recipes in the Answers to Correspondents.

When I was quite a young man I used to sit in dark corners and listen, with swelling heart, while people at the piano told me where little girl babies got their wonderful eyes from, of the things they did to them in heaven that gave them dimples. Ah me! I wish now I had never come across those ladies' papers. I know the stuff that causes those bewitching eyes. I know the shop where they make those dimples; I have passed it and looked in. I thought they were produced by angels' kisses, but there was not an angel about the place, that I could see. Perhaps I have also been deceived as regards their goodness. Maybe all women are not so perfect as in the popular short story they appear to be. That is why I suggest that Science should proceed still further, and make them all as beautiful in mind as she is now able to make them in body. May we not live to see in the advertisement columns of the ladies' paper of the future the portrait of a young girl sulking in a corner—"Before taking the lotion!" The same girl dancing among her little brothers and sisters, shedding sunlight through the home—"After the three first bottles!" May we not have the Caudle Mixture: One tablespoonful at bed-time guaranteed to make the lady murmur, "Good-night, dear; hope you'll sleep well," and at once to fall asleep, her lips parted in a smile? Maybe some specialist of the future will advertise Mind Massage: "Warranted to remove from the most obstinate subject all traces of hatred, envy, and malice."

And, when Science has done everything possible for women, there might be no harm in her turning her attention to us men. Her idea at present seems to be that we men are too beautiful, physically and morally, to need improvement. Personally, there are one or two points about which I should like to consult her.

WHEN IS THE BEST TIME TO BE MERRY?

There is so much I could do to improve things generally in and about Europe, if only I had a free hand. I should not propose any great fundamental changes. These poor people have got used to their own ways; it would be unwise to reform them all at once. But there are many little odds and ends that I could do for them, so many of their mistakes I could correct for them. They do not know this. If they only knew there was a man living in their midst willing to take them in hand and arrange things for them, how glad they would be. But the story is always the same. One reads it in the advertisements of the matrimonial column:

"A lady, young, said to be good-looking"—she herself is not sure on the point; she feels that possibly she may be prejudiced; she puts before you merely the current gossip of the neighbourhood; people say she is beautiful; they may be right, they may be wrong: it is not for her to decide—"well-educated, of affectionate disposition, possessed of means, desires to meet gentleman with a view to matrimony."

Immediately underneath one reads of a gentleman of twenty-eight, "tall, fair, considered agreeable." Really the modesty of the matrimonial advertiser teaches to us ordinary mortals quite a beautiful lesson. I know instinctively that were anybody to ask me suddenly:

"Do you call yourself an agreeable man?" I should answer promptly:

"An agreeable man! Of course I'm an agreeable man. What silly questions you do ask!" If he persisted in arguing the matter, saying:

"But there are people who do not consider you an agreeable man." I should get angry with him.

"Oh, they think that, do they?" I should say. "Well, you tell them from me, with my compliments, that they are a set of blithering idiots. Not agreeable! You show me the man who says I'm not agreeable. I'll soon let him know whether I'm agreeable or not."

These young men seeking a wife are silent on the subject of their own virtues. Such are for others to discover. The matrimonial advertiser confines himself to a simple statement of fact: he is considered agreeable."

He is domestically inclined, and in receipt of a good income. He is desirous of meeting a lady of serious disposition, with view to matrimony. If possessed of means—well, it is a trifle hardly worth considering one way or the other. He does not insist upon it; on the other hand he does not exclude ladies of means; the main idea is matrimony.

It is sad to reflect upon a young lady, said to be good-looking (let us say good-looking and be done with it: a neighbourhood does not rise up and declare a girl good-looking if she is not good-looking, that is only her modest way of putting it), let us say a young lady, good-looking, well-educated, of affectionate disposition—it is undeniably sad to reflect that such an one, matrimonially inclined, should be compelled to have recourse to the columns of a matrimonial journal. What are the young men in the neighbourhood thinking of? What more do they want? Is it Venus come to life again with ten thousand a year that they are waiting for! It makes me angry with my own sex reading these advertisements. And when one thinks of the girls that do get married!

But life is a mystery. The fact remains: here is the ideal wife seeking in vain for a husband. And here, immediately underneath—I will not say the ideal husband, he may have faults; none of us are perfect, but as men go a decided acquisition to any domestic hearth, an agreeable gentleman, fond of home life, none of your gad-abouts— calls aloud to the four winds for a wife—any sort of a wife, provided she be of a serious disposition. In his despair, he has grown indifferent to all other considerations. "Is there in this world," he has said to himself, "one unmarried woman, willing to marry me, an agreeable man, in receipt of a good income." Possibly enough this twain have passed one another in the street, have sat side by side in the same tram-car, never guessing, each one, that the other was the very article of which they were in want to make life beautiful.

Mistresses in search of a servant, not so much with the idea of getting work out of her, rather with the object of making her happy, advertise on one page. On the opposite page, domestic treasures— disciples of Carlyle, apparently, with a passionate love of work for its own sake—are seeking situations, not so much with the desire of gain as with the hope of finding openings where they may enjoy the luxury of feeling they are leading useful lives. These philanthropic mistresses, these toil-loving hand-maidens, have lived side by side in the same town for years, never knowing one another.

So it is with these poor European peoples. They pass me in the street. They do not guess that I am ready and willing to take them under my care, to teach them common sense with a smattering of intelligence—to be, as one might say, a father to them. They look at me. There is nothing about me to tell them that I know what is good for them better than they do themselves. In the fairy tales the wise man wore a conical hat and a long robe with twiddly things all round the edge. You knew he was a clever man. It avoided the necessity of explanation. Unfortunately, the fashion has gone out. We wise men have to wear just ordinary clothes. Nobody knows we are wise men. Even when we tell them so, they don't believe it. This it is that makes our task the more difficult.

One of the first things I should take in hand, were European affairs handed over to my control, would be the rearrangement of the Carnival. As matters are, the Carnival takes place all over Europe in February. At Nice, in Spain, or in Italy, it may be occasionally possible to feel you want to dance about the streets in thin costume during February. But in more northern countries during Carnival time I have seen only one sensible masker; he was a man who had got himself up as a diver. It was in Antwerp. The rain was pouring down in torrents; a cheery, boisterous John Bull sort of an east wind was blustering through the streets at the rate of fifteen miles an hour. Pierrots, with frozen hands, were blowing blue noses. An elderly Cupid had borrowed an umbrella from a cafe and was waiting for a tram. A very little devil was crying with the cold, and wiping his eyes with the end of his own tail. Every doorway was crowded with shivering maskers. The diver alone walked erect, the water streaming from him.

February is not the month for open air masquerading. The "confetti," which has come to be nothing but coloured paper cut into small discs, is a sodden mass. When a lump of it strikes you in the eye, your instinct is not to laugh gaily, but to find out the man who threw it and to hit him back. This is not the true spirit of Carnival. The marvel is that, in spite of the almost invariably adverse weather, these Carnivals still continue. In Belgium, where Romanism still remains the dominant religion, Carnival maintains itself stronger than elsewhere in Northern Europe.

At one small town, Binche, near the French border, it holds uninterrupted sway for three days and two nights, during which time the whole of the population, swelled by visitors from twenty miles round, shouts, romps, eats and drinks and dances. After which the visitors are packed like sardines into railway trains. They pin their tickets to their coats and promptly go to sleep. At every station the railway officials stumble up and down the trains with lanterns. The last feeble effort of the more wakeful reveller, before he adds himself to the heap of snoring humanity on the floor of the railway carriage, is to change the tickets of a couple of his unconscious companions. In this way gentlemen for the east are dragged out by the legs at junctions, and packed into trains going west; while southern fathers are shot out in the chill dawn at lonely northern stations, to find themselves greeted with enthusiasm by other people's families.

At Binche, they say—I have not counted them myself—that thirty thousand maskers can be seen dancing at the same time. When they are not dancing they are throwing oranges at one another. The houses board up their windows. The restaurants take down their mirrors and hide away the glasses. If I went masquerading at Binche I should go as a man in armour, period Henry the Seventh.

"Doesn't it hurt," I asked a lady who had been there, "having oranges thrown at you? Which sort do they use, speaking generally, those fine juicy ones—Javas I think you call them—or the little hard brand with skins like a nutmeg-grater? And if both sorts are used indiscriminately, which do you personally prefer?"

"The smart people," she answered, "they are the same everywhere—they must be extravagant—they use the Java orange. If it hits you in the back I prefer the Java orange. It is more messy than the other, but it does not leave you with that curious sensation of having been temporarily stunned. Most people, of course, make use of the small hard orange. If you duck in time, and so catch it on the top of your head, it does not hurt so much as you would think. If, however, it hits you on a tender place—well, myself, I always find that a little sal volatile, with old cognac—half and half, you understand—is about the best thing. But it only happens once a year," she added.

Nearly every town gives prizes for the best group of maskers. In some cases the first prize amounts to as much as two hundred pounds. The butchers, the bakers, the candlestick makers, join together and compete. They arrive in wagons, each group with its band. Free trade is encouraged. Each neighbouring town and village "dumps" its load of picturesque merry-makers.

It is in these smaller towns that the spirit of King Carnival finds happiest expression. Almost every third inhabitant takes part in the fun. In Brussels and the larger towns the thing appears ridiculous. A few hundred maskers force their way with difficulty through thousands of dull-clad spectators, looking like a Spanish river in the summer time, a feeble stream, dribbling through acres of muddy bank. At Charleroi, the centre of the Belgian Black Country, the chief feature of the Carnival is the dancing of the children. A space is specially roped off for them.

If by chance the sun is kind enough to shine, the sight is a pretty one. How they love the dressing up and the acting, these small mites! One young hussy—she could hardly have been more than ten— was gotten up as a haughty young lady. Maybe some elder sister had served as a model. She wore a tremendous wig of flaxen hair, a hat that I guarantee would have made its mark even at Ascot on the Cup Day, a skirt that trailed two yards behind her, a pair of what had once been white kid gloves, and a blue silk parasol. Dignity! I have seen the offended barmaid, I have met the chorus girl—not by appointment, please don't misunderstand me, merely as a spectator—up the river on Sunday. But never have I witnessed in any human being so much hauteur to the pound avoir-dupois as was carried through the streets of Charleroi by that small brat. Companions of other days, mere vulgar boys and girls, claimed acquaintance with her. She passed them with a stare of such utter disdain that it sent them tumbling over one another backwards. By the time they had recovered themselves sufficiently to think of an old tin kettle lying handy in the gutter she had turned the corner.

Two miserably clad urchins, unable to scrape together the few sous necessary for the hire of a rag or two, had nevertheless determined not to be altogether out of it. They had managed to borrow a couple of white blouses—not what you would understand by a white blouse, dear Madame, a dainty thing of frills and laces, but the coarse white sack the street sweeper wears over his clothes. They had also borrowed a couple of brooms. Ridiculous little objects they looked, the tiny head of each showing above the great white shroud as gravely they walked, the one behind the other, sweeping the mud into the gutter. They also were of the Carnival, playing at being scavengers.

Another quaint sight I witnessed. The "serpentin" is a feature of the Belgian Carnival. It is a strip of coloured paper, some dozen yards long, perhaps. You fling it as you would a lassoo, entangling the head of some passer-by. Naturally, the object most aimed at by the Belgian youth is the Belgian maiden. And, naturally also, the maiden who finds herself most entangled is the maiden who—to use again the language of the matrimonial advertiser—"is considered good-looking." The serpentin about her head is the "feather in her cap" of the Belgian maiden on Carnival Day. Coming suddenly round the corner I almost ran into a girl. Her back was towards me. It was a quiet street. She had half a dozen of these serpentins. Hurriedly, with trembling hands, she was twisting them round and round her own head. I looked at her as I passed. She flushed scarlet. Poor little snub-nosed pasty-faced woman! I wish she had not seen me. I could have bought sixpenny-worth, followed her, and tormented her with them; while she would have pretended indignation— sought, discreetly, to escape from me.

Down South, where the blood flows quicker, King Carnival is, indeed, a jolly old soul. In Munich he reigns for six weeks, the end coming with a mad two days revel in the streets. During the whole of the period, folks in ordinary, every-day costume are regarded as curiosities; people wonder what they are up to. From the Grafin to the Dienstmadchen, from the Herr Professor to the "Piccolo," as they term the small artist that answers to our page boy, the business of Munich is dancing, somewhere, somehow, in a fancy costume. Every theatre clears away the stage, every cafe crowds its chairs and tables into corners, the very streets are cleared for dancing. Munich goes mad.

Munich is always a little mad. The maddest ball I ever danced at was in Munich. I went there with a Harvard University professor. He had been told what these balls were like. Ever seeking knowledge of all things, he determined to take the matter up for himself and examine it. The writer also must ever be learning. I agreed to accompany him. We had not intended to dance. Our idea was that we could be indulgent spectators, regarding from some coign of vantage the antics of the foolish crowd. The professor was clad as became a professor. Myself, I wore a simply-cut frock-coat, with trousering in French grey. The doorkeeper explained to us that this was a costume ball; he was sorry, but gentlemen could only be admitted in evening dress or in masquerade.

It was half past one in the morning. We had sat up late on purpose; we had gone without our dinner; we had walked two miles. The professor suggested pinning up the tails of his clerically-cut coat and turning in his waistcoat. The doorkeeper feared it would not be quite the same thing. Besides, my French grey trousers refused to adapt themselves. The doorkeeper proposed our hiring a costume—a little speculation of his own; gentlemen found it simpler sometimes, especially married gentlemen, to hire a costume in this manner, changing back into sober garments before returning home. It reduced the volume of necessary explanation.

"Have you anything, my good man," said the professor, "anything that would effect a complete disguise?"

The doorkeeper had the very thing—a Chinese arrangement, with combined mask and wig. It fitted neatly over the head, and was provided with a simple but ingenious piece of mechanism by means of which much could be done with the pigtail. Myself the doorkeeper hid from view under the cowl of a Carmelite monk.

"I do hope nobody recognises us," whispered my friend the professor as we entered.

I can only hope sincerely that they did not. I do not wish to talk about myself. That would be egotism. But the mystery of the professor troubles me to this day. A grave, earnest gentleman, the father of a family, I saw him with my own eyes put that ridiculous pasteboard mask over his head. Later on—a good deal later on—I found myself walking again with him through silent star-lit streets. Where he had been in the interval, and who then was the strange creature under the Chinaman's mask, will always remain to me an unsolved problem.

DO WE LIE A-BED TOO LATE?

It was in Paris, many years ago, that I fell by chance into this habit of early rising. My night—by reasons that I need not enter into—had been a troubled one. Tired of the hot bed that gave no sleep, I rose and dressed myself, crept down the creaking stairs, experiencing the sensations of a burglar new to his profession, unbolted the great door of the hotel, and passed out into an unknown, silent city, bathed in a mysterious soft light. Since then, this strange sweet city of the dawn has never ceased to call to me. It may be in London, in Paris again, in Brussels, Berlin, Vienna, that I have gone to sleep, but if perchance I wake before the returning tide of human life has dimmed its glories with the mists and vapours of the noisy day, I know that beyond my window blind the fairy city, as I saw it first so many years ago—this city that knows no tears, no sorrow, through which there creeps no evil thing; this city of quiet vistas, fading into hope; this city of far-off voices whispering peace; this city of the dawn that still is young—invites me to talk with it awhile before the waking hours drive it before them, and with a sigh it passes whence it came.

It is the great city's one hour of purity, of dignity. The very rag-picker, groping with her filthy hands among the ashes, instead of an object of contempt, moves from door to door an accusing Figure, her thin soiled garments, her bent body, her scarred face, hideous with the wounds of poverty, an eloquent indictment of smug Injustice, sleeping behind its deaf shutters. Yet even into her dim brain has sunk the peace that fills for this brief hour the city. This, too, shall have its end, my sister! Men and women were not born to live on the husks that fill the pails outside the rich man's door. Courage a little while longer, you and yours. Your rheumy eyes once were bright, your thin locks once soft and wavy, your poor bent back once straight; and maybe, as they tell you in their gilded churches, this bulging sack shall be lifted from your weary shoulders, your misshapen limbs be straight again. You pass not altogether unheeded through these empty streets. Not all the eyes of the universe are sleeping.

The little seamstress, hurrying to her early work! A little later she will be one of the foolish crowd, joining in the foolish laughter, in the coarse jests of the work-room: but as yet the hot day has not claimed her. The work-room is far beyond, the home of mean cares and sordid struggles far behind. To her, also, in this moment are the sweet thoughts of womanhood. She puts down her bag, rests herself upon a seat. If all the day were dawn, this city of the morning always with us! A neighbouring clock chimes forth the hour. She starts up from her dream and hurries on—to the noisy work-room.

A pair of lovers cross the park, holding each other's hands. They will return later in the day, but there will be another expression in their eyes, another meaning in the pressure of their hands. Now the purity of the morning is with them.

Some fat, middle-aged clerk comes puffing into view: his ridiculous little figure very podgy. He stops to take off his hat and mop his bald head with his handkerchief: even to him the morning lends romance. His fleshy face changes almost as one looks at him. One sees again the lad with his vague hopes, his absurd ambitions.

There is a statue of Aphrodite in one of the smaller Paris parks. Twice in the same week, without particularly meaning it, I found myself early in the morning standing in front of this statue gazing listlessly at it, as one does when in dreamy mood; and on both occasions, turning to go, I encountered the same man, also gazing at it with, apparently, listless eyes. He was an uninteresting looking man—possibly he thought the same of me. From his dress he might have been a well-to-do tradesman, a minor Government official, doctor, or lawyer. Quite ten years later I paid my third visit to the same statue at about the same hour. This time he was there before me. I was hidden from him by some bushes. He glanced round but did not see me; and then he did a curious thing. Placing his hands on the top of the pedestal, which may have been some seven feet in height, he drew himself up, and kissed very gently, almost reverentially, the foot of the statue, begrimed though it was with the city's dirt. Had he been some long-haired student of the Latin Quarter one would not have been so astonished. But he was such a very commonplace, quite respectable looking man. Afterwards he drew a pipe

26

from his pocket, carefully filled and lighted it, took his umbrella from the seat where it had been lying, and walked away.

Had it been their meeting-place long ago? Had he been wont to tell her, gazing at her with lover's eyes, how like she was to the statue? The French sculptor has not to consider Mrs. Grundy. Maybe, the lady, raising her eyes, had been confused; perhaps for a moment angry—some little milliner or governess, one supposes. In France the jeune fille of good family does not meet her lover unattended. What had happened? Or was it but the vagrant fancy of a middle-aged bourgeois seeking in imagination the romance that reality so rarely gives us, weaving his love dream round his changeless statue?

In one of Ibsen's bitter comedies the lovers agree to part while they are still young, never to see each other in the flesh again. Into the future each will bear away the image of the other, godlike, radiant with the glory of youth and love; each will cherish the memory of a loved one who shall be beautiful always. That their parting may not appear such wild nonsense as at first it strikes us, Ibsen shows us other lovers who have married in the orthodox fashion. She was all that a mistress should be. They speak of her as they first knew her fifteen years ago, when every man was at her feet. He then was a young student, burning with fine ideals, with enthusiasm for all the humanities.

They enter.

What did you expect? Fifteen years have passed—fifteen years of struggle with the grim realities. He is fat and bald. Eleven children have to be provided for. High ideals will not even pay the bootmaker. To exist you have to fight for mean ends with mean weapons. And the sweet girl heroine! Now the worried mother of eleven brats! One rings down the curtain amid Satanic laughter.

That is why, for one reason among so many, I love this mystic morning light. It has a strange power of revealing the beauty that is hidden from us by the coarser beams of the full day. These worn men and women, grown so foolish looking, so unromantic; these artisans and petty clerks plodding to their monotonous day's work; these dull-eyed women of the people on their way to market to haggle over sous, to argue and contend over paltry handfuls of food. In this magic morning light the disguising body becomes transparent. They have grown beautiful, not ugly, with the years of toil and hardship; these lives, lived so patiently, are consecrated to the service of the world. Joy, hope, pleasure—they have done with all such, life for them is over. Yet they labour, ceaselessly, uncomplainingly. It is for the children.

One morning, near Brussels, I encountered a cart of faggots, drawn by a hound so lean that stroking him might have hurt a dainty hand. I was shocked—angry, till I noticed his fellow beast of burden pushing the cart from behind. Such a scarecrow of an old woman! There was little to choose between them. I walked with them a little way. She lived near Waterloo. All day she gathered wood in the great forest, and starting at three o'clock each morning, the two lean creatures between them dragged the cart nine miles to Brussels, returning when they had sold their load. With luck she might reckon on a couple of francs. I asked her if she could not find something else to do.

Yes, it was possible, but for the little one, her grandchild. Folks will not employ old women burdened with grandchildren.

You fair, dainty ladies, who would never know it was morning if somebody did not enter to pull up the blind and tell you so! You do well not to venture out in this magic morning light. You would look so plain—almost ugly, by the side of these beautiful women.

It is curious the attraction the Church has always possessed for the marketing classes. Christ drove them from the Temple, but still, in every continental city, they cluster round its outer walls. It makes a charming picture on a sunny morning, the great cathedral with its massive shadow forming the background; splashed about its feet, like a parterre of gay flowers around the trunk of some old tree, the women, young girls in their many coloured costumes, sitting before their piled-up baskets of green vegetables, of shining fruits.

In Brussels the chief market is held on the Grande Place. The great gilded houses have looked down upon much the same scene every morning these four hundred years. In summer time it commences about half-past four; by five o'clock it is a roaring hive, the great city round about still sleeping.

Here comes the thrifty housewife of the poor, to whom the difference of a tenth of a penny in the price of a cabbage is all-important, and the much harassed keeper of the petty pension. There are houses in Brussels where they will feed you, light you, sleep you, wait on you, for two francs a day. Withered old ladies, ancient governesses, who will teach you for forty centimes an hour, gather round these ricketty tables, wolf up the thin soup, grumble at the watery coffee, help themselves with unladylike greediness to the potato pie. It must need careful housewifery to keep these poor creatures on two francs a day and make a profit for yourself. So "Madame," the much-grumbled-at, who has gone to bed about twelve, rises a little before five, makes her way down with her basket. Thus a few sous may be saved upon the day's economies.

Sometimes it is a mere child who is the little housekeeper. One thinks that perhaps this early training in the art of haggling may not be good for her. Already there is a hard expression in the childish eyes, mean lines about the little mouth. The finer qualities of humanity are expensive luxuries, not to be afforded by the poor.

They overwork their patient dogs, and underfeed them. During the two hours' market the poor beasts, still fastened to their little "chariots," rest in the open space about the neighbouring Bourse. They snatch at what you throw them; they do not even thank you with a wag of the tail. Gratitude! Politeness! What mean you? We have not heard of such. We only work. Some of them amid all the din lie sleeping between their shafts. Some are licking one another's sores. One would they were better treated; alas! their owners, likewise, are overworked and underfed, housed in kennels no better. But if the majority in every society were not overworked and underfed and meanly housed, why, then the minority could not be underworked and overfed and housed luxuriously. But this is talk to which no respectable reader can be expected to listen.

They are one babel of bargaining, these markets. The purchaser selects a cauliflower. Fortunately, cauliflowers have no feelings, or probably it would burst into tears at the expression with which it is regarded. It is impossible that any lady should desire such a cauliflower. Still, out of mere curiosity, she would know the price—that is, if the owner of the cauliflower is not too much ashamed of it to name a price.

The owner of the cauliflower suggests six sous. The thing is too ridiculous for argument. The purchaser breaks into a laugh.

The owner of the cauliflower is stung. She points out the beauties of that cauliflower. Apparently it is the cauliflower out of all her stock she loves the best; a better cauliflower never lived; if there were more cauliflowers in the world like this particular cauliflower things might be different. She gives a sketch of the cauliflower's career, from its youth upwards. Hard enough it will be for her when the hour for parting from it comes. If the other lady has not sufficient knowledge of cauliflowers to appreciate it, will she kindly not paw it about, but put it down and go away, and never let the owner of the cauliflower see her again.

The other lady, more as a friend than as a purchaser, points out the cauliflower's defects. She wishes well to the owner of the cauliflower, and would like to teach her something about her business. A lady who thinks such a cauliflower worth six sous can never hope to succeed as a cauliflower vendor. Has she really taken the trouble to examine the cauliflower for herself, or has love made her blind to its shortcomings?

The owner of the cauliflower is too indignant to reply. She snatches it away, appears to be comforting it, replaces it in the basket. The other lady is grieved at human obstinacy and stupidity in general. If the owner of the cauliflower had had any sense she would have asked four sous. Eventually business is done at five.

It is the custom everywhere abroad—asking the price of a thing is simply opening conversation. A lady told me that, the first day she began housekeeping in Florence, she handed over to a poulterer for a chicken the price he had demanded—with protestations that he was losing on the transaction, but wanted, for family reasons, apparently, to get rid of the chicken. He stood for half a minute staring at her, and then, being an honest sort of man, threw in a pigeon.

Foreign housekeepers starting business in London appear hurt when our tradesmen decline to accept half-a-crown for articles marked three-and-six.

"Then why mark it only three-and-sixpence?" is the foreign housekeeper's argument.

SHOULD MARRIED MEN PLAY GOLF?

That we Englishmen attach too much importance to sport goes without saying—or, rather, it has been said so often as to have become a commonplace. One of these days some reforming English novelist will write a book, showing the evil effects of over-indulgence in sport: the neglected business, the ruined home, the slow but sure sapping of the brain—what there may have been of it in the beginning—leading to semi-imbecility and yearly increasing obesity.

A young couple, I once heard of, went for their honeymoon to Scotland. The poor girl did not know he was a golfer (he had wooed and won her during a period of idleness enforced by a sprained shoulder), or maybe she would have avoided Scotland. The idea they started with was that of a tour. The second day the man went out for a stroll by himself. At dinner-time he observed, with a far-away look in his eyes, that it seemed a pretty spot they had struck, and suggested their staying there another day. The next morning after breakfast he borrowed a club from the hotel porter, and remarked that he would take a walk while she finished doing her hair. He said it amused him, swinging a club while he walked. He returned in time for lunch and seemed moody all the afternoon. He said the air suited him, and urged that they should linger yet another day.

She was young and inexperienced, and thought, maybe, it was liver. She had heard much about liver from her father. The next morning he borrowed more clubs, and went out, this time before breakfast, returning to a late and not over sociable dinner. That was the end of their honeymoon so far as she was concerned. He meant well, but the thing had gone too far. The vice had entered into his blood, and the smell of the links drove out all other considerations.

We are most of us familiar, I take it, with the story of the golfing parson, who could not keep from swearing when the balls went wrong.

"Golf and the ministry don't seem to go together," his friend told him. "Take my advice before it's too late, and give it up, Tammas."

A few months later Tammas met his friend again.

"You were right, Jamie," cried the parson cheerily, "they didna run well in harness; golf and the meenistry, I hae followed your advice: I hae gi'en it oop."

"Then what are ye doing with that sack of clubs?" inquired Jamie.

"What am I doing with them?" repeated the puzzled Tammas. "Why I am going to play golf with them." A light broke upon him. "Great Heavens, man!" he continued, "ye didna' think 'twas the golf I'd gi'en oop?"

The Englishman does not understand play. He makes a life-long labour of his sport, and to it sacrifices mind and body. The health resorts of Europe—to paraphrase a famous saying that nobody appears to have said—draw half their profits from the playing fields of Eton and elsewhere. In Swiss and German kurhausen enormously fat men bear down upon you and explain to you that once they were the champion sprinters or the high-jump representatives of their university—men who now hold on to the bannisters and groan as they haul themselves upstairs. Consumptive men, between paroxysms of coughing, tell you of the goals they scored when they were half-backs or forwards of extraordinary ability. Ex-light-weight amateur pugilists, with the figure now of an American roll-top desk, butt you into a corner of the billiard-room, and, surprised they cannot get as near you as they would desire, whisper to you the secret of avoiding the undercut by the swiftness of the backward leap. Broken-down tennis players, one-legged skaters, dropsical gentlemen-riders, are to be met with hobbling on crutches along every highway of the Engadine.

They are pitiable objects. Never having learnt to read anything but the sporting papers, books are of no use to them. They never wasted much of their youth on thought, and, apparently, have lost the knack of it. They don't care for art, and Nature only suggests to them the things they can no longer do. The snow-clad mountain reminds them that once they were daring tobogannists; the undulating common makes them sad because they can no longer handle a golf-club; by the riverside they sit down and tell you of the salmon they caught before they caught rheumatic fever; birds only make them long for guns; music raises visions of the local cricket-match of long ago, enlivened by the local band; a picturesque estaminet, with little tables spread out under the vines, recalls bitter memories of ping-pong. One is sorry for them, but their conversation is not exhilarating. The man who has other interests in life beyond sport is apt to find their reminiscences monotonous; while to one another they do not care to talk. One gathers that they do not altogether believe one another.

The foreigner is taking kindly to our sports; one hopes he will be forewarned by our example and not overdo the thing. At present, one is bound to admit, he shows no sign of taking sport too seriously. Football is gaining favour more and more throughout Europe. But yet the Frenchman has not got it out of his head that the coup to practise is kicking the ball high into the air and catching it upon his head. He would rather catch the ball upon his head than score a goal. If he can manoeuvre the ball away into a corner, kick it up into the air twice running, and each time catch it on his head, he does not seem to care what happens after that. Anybody can have the ball; he has had his game and is happy.

They talk of introducing cricket into Belgium; I shall certainly try to be present at the opening game. I am afraid that, until he learns from experience, the Belgian fielder will stop cricket balls with his head. That the head is the proper thing with which to play ball appears to be in his blood. My head is round, he argues, and hard, just like the ball itself; what part of the human frame more fit and proper with which to meet and stop a ball.

Golf has not yet caught on, but tennis is firmly established from St. Petersburg to Bordeaux. The German, with the thoroughness characteristic of him, is working hard. University professors, stout majors, rising early in the morning, hire boys and practise back-handers and half-volleys. But to the Frenchman, as yet, it is a game. He plays it in a happy, merry fashion, that is shocking to English eyes.

Your partner's service rather astonishes you. An occasional yard or so beyond the line happens to anyone, but this man's object appears to be to break windows. You feel you really must remonstrate, when the joyous laughter and tumultuous applause of the spectators explain the puzzle to you. He has not been trying to serve; he has been trying to hit a man in the next court who is stooping down to tie up his shoe-lace. With his last ball he has succeeded. He has hit the man in the small of the back, and has bowled him over. The unanimous opinion of the surrounding critics is that the ball could not possibly have been better placed. A Doherty has never won greater applause from the crowd. Even the man who has been hit appears pleased; it shows what a Frenchman can do when he does take up a game.

But French honour demands revenge. He forgets his shoe, he forgets his game. He gathers together all the balls that he can find; his balls, your balls, anybody's balls that happen to be handy. And then commences the return match. At this point it is best to crouch down under shelter of the net. Most of the players round about adopt this plan; the more timid make for the club-house, and, finding themselves there, order coffee and light up cigarettes. After a while both players appear to be satisfied. The other players then gather round to claim their balls. This makes a good game by itself. The object is to get as many balls as you can, your own and other people's—for preference other people's—and run off with them round the courts, followed by whooping claimants.

In the course of half-an-hour or so, when everybody is dead beat, the game—the original game—is resumed. You demand the score; your partner promptly says it is "forty-fifteen." Both your opponents rush up to the net, and apparently there is going to be a duel. It is only a friendly altercation; they very much doubt its being "forty-fifteen." "Fifteen-forty" they could believe; they suggest it as a compromise. The discussion is concluded by calling it deuce. As it is rare for a game to proceed without some such incident occurring in the middle of it, the score generally is deuce. This avoids heart-burning; nobody wins a set and nobody loses. The one game generally suffices for the afternoon.

To the earnest player, it is also confusing to miss your partner occasionally—to turn round and find that he is talking to a man. Nobody but yourself takes the slightest objection to his absence. The other side appear to regard it as a good opportunity to score. Five minutes later he resumes the game. His friend comes with him, also the dog of his friend. The dog is welcomed with enthusiasm; all balls are returned to the dog. Until the dog is tired you do not get a look in. But all this will no doubt soon be changed. There are some excellent French and Belgian players; from them their compatriots will gradually learn higher ideals. The Frenchman is young in the game. As the right conception of the game grows upon him, he will also learn to keep the balls lower.

I suppose it is the continental sky. It is so blue, so beautiful; it naturally attracts one. Anyhow, the fact remains that most tennis players on the Continent, whether English or foreign, have a tendency to aim the ball direct at Heaven. At an English club in Switzerland there existed in my days a young Englishman who was really a wonderful player. To get the ball past him was almost an impossibility. It was his return that was weak. He only had one stroke; the ball went a hundred feet or so into the air and descended in his opponent's court. The other man would stand watching it, a little speck in the Heavens, growing gradually bigger and bigger as it neared the earth. Newcomers would chatter to him, thinking he had detected a balloon or an eagle. He would wave them aside, explain to them that he would talk to them later, after the arrival of the ball. It would fall with a thud at his feet, rise another twenty yards or so and again descend. When it was at the proper height he would hit it back over the net, and the next moment it would be mounting the sky again. At tournaments I have seen that young man, with tears in his eyes, pleading to be given an umpire. Every umpire had fled. They hid behind trees, borrowed silk hats and umbrellas and pretended they were visitors—any device, however mean, to avoid the task of umpiring for that young man. Provided his opponent did not go to sleep or get cramp, one game might last all day. Anyone could return his balls; but, as I have said, to get a ball past him was almost an impossibility. He invariably won; the other man, after an hour or so, would get mad and try to lose. It was his only chance of dinner.

It is a pretty sight, generally speaking, a tennis ground abroad. The women pay more attention to their costumes than do our lady players. The men are usually in spotless white. The ground is often charmingly situated, the club-house picturesque; there is always laughter and merriment. The play may not be so good to watch, but the picture is delightful. I accompanied a man a little while ago to his club on the outskirts of Brussels. The ground was bordered by a wood on one side, and surrounded on the other three by petites fermes—allotments, as we should call them in England, worked by the peasants themselves.

It was a glorious spring afternoon. The courts were crowded. The red earth and the green grass formed a background against which the women, in their new Parisian toilets, under their bright parasols, stood out like wondrous bouquets of moving flowers. The whole atmosphere was a delightful mingling of idle gaiety, flirtation, and graceful sensuousness. A modern Watteau would have seized upon the scene with avidity.

Just beyond—separated by the almost invisible wire fencing—a group of peasants were working in the field. An old woman and a young girl, with ropes about their shoulders, were drawing a harrow, guided by a withered old scarecrow of a man. They paused for a moment at the wire fencing, and looked through. It was an odd contrast; the two worlds divided by that wire fencing—so slight, almost invisible. The girl swept the sweat from her face with her hand; the woman pushed back her grey locks underneath the handkerchief knotted about her head; the old man straightened himself with some difficulty. So they stood, for perhaps a minute, gazing with quiet, passionless faces through that slight fencing, that a push from their work-hardened hands might have levelled.

Was there any thought, I wonder, passing through their brains? The young girl—she was a handsome creature in spite of her disfiguring garments. The woman—it was a wonderfully fine face: clear, calm eyes, deep-set under a square broad brow. The withered old scarecrow—ever sowing the seed in the spring of the fruit that others shall eat.

The old man bent again over the guiding ropes: gave the word. The team moved forward up the hill. It is Anatole France, I think, who says: Society is based upon the patience of the poor.

ARE EARLY MARRIAGES A MISTAKE?

I am chary nowadays of offering counsel in connection with subjects concerning which I am not and cannot be an authority. Long ago I once took upon myself to write a paper about babies. It did not aim to be a textbook on the subject. It did not even claim to exhaust the topic. I was willing that others, coming after me, should continue the argument— that is if, upon reflection, they were still of opinion there was anything more to be said. I was pleased with the article. I went out of my way to obtain an early copy of the magazine in which it appeared, on purpose to show it to a lady friend of mine. She was the possessor of one or two babies of her own, specimens in no way remarkable, though she herself, as was natural enough, did her best to boom them. I thought it might be helpful to her: the views and observations, not of a rival fancier, who would be prejudiced, but of an intelligent amateur. I put the magazine into her hands, opened at the proper place.

"Read it through carefully and quietly," I said; "don't let anything distract you. Have a pencil and a bit of paper ready at your side, and note down any points upon which you would like further information. If there is anything you think I have missed out let me know. It may be that here and there you will be disagreeing with me. If so, do not hesitate to mention it, I shall not be angry. If a demand arises I shall very likely issue an enlarged and improved edition of this paper in the form of a pamphlet, in which case hints and suggestions that to you may appear almost impertinent will be of distinct help to me."

"I haven't got a pencil," she said; "what's it all about?"

"It's about babies," I explained, and I lent her a pencil.

That is another thing I have learnt. Never lend a pencil to a woman if you ever want to see it again. She has three answers to your request for its return. The first, that she gave it back to you and that you put it in your pocket, and that it's there now, and that if it isn't it ought to be. The second, that you never lent it to her. The third, that she wishes people would not lend her pencils and then clamour for them back, just when she has something else far more important to think about.

"What do you know about babies?" she demanded.

"If you will read the paper," I replied, "you will see for yourself. It's all there."

She flicked over the pages contemptuously.

"There doesn't seem much of it?" she retorted.

"It is condensed," I pointed out to her.

"I am glad it is short. All right, I'll read it," she agreed.

I thought my presence might disturb her, so went out into the garden. I wanted her to get the full benefit of it. I crept back now and again to peep through the open window. She did not seem to be making many notes. But I heard her making little noises to herself. When I saw she had reached the last page, I re-entered the room.

"Well?" I said.

"Is it meant to be funny," she demanded, "or is it intended to be taken seriously?"

"There may be flashes of humour here and there—"

She did not wait for me to finish.

"Because if it's meant to be funny," she said, "I don't think it is at all funny. And if it is intended to be serious, there's one thing very clear, and that is that you are not a mother."

With the unerring instinct of the born critic she had divined my one weak point. Other objections raised against me I could have met. But that one stinging reproach was unanswerable. It has made me, as I have explained, chary of tendering advice on matters outside my own department of life. Otherwise, every year, about Valentine's day, there is much that I should like to say to my good friends the birds. I want to put it to them seriously. Is not the month of February just a little too early? Of course, their answer would be the same as in the case of my motherly friend.

"Oh, what do you know about it? you are not a bird."

I know I am not a bird, but that is the very reason why they should listen to me. I bring a fresh mind to bear upon the subject. I am not tied down by bird convention. February, my dear friends—in these northern climes of ours at all events—is much too early. You have to build in a high wind, and nothing, believe me, tries a lady's temper more than being blown about. Nature is nature, and womenfolk, my dear sirs, are the same all the world over, whether they be birds or whether they be human. I am an older person than most of you, and I speak with the weight of experience.

If I were going to build a house with my wife, I should not choose a season of the year when the bricks and planks and things were liable to be torn out of her hand, her skirts blown over her head, and she left clinging for dear life to a scaffolding pole. I know the feminine biped and, you take it from me, that is not her notion of a honeymoon. In April or May, the sun shining, the air balmy—when, after carrying up to her a load or two of bricks, and a hod or two of mortar, we could knock off work for a few minutes without fear of the whole house being swept away into the next street—could sit side by side on the top of a wall, our legs dangling down, and peck and morsel together; after which I could whistle a bit to her—then housebuilding might be a pleasure.

The swallows are wisest; June is their idea, and a very good idea, too. In a mountain village in the Tyrol, early one summer, I had the opportunity of watching very closely the building of a swallow's nest. After coffee, the first morning, I stepped out from the great, cool, dark passage of the wirtschaft into the blazing sunlight, and, for no particular reason, pulled-to the massive door behind me. While filling my pipe, a swallow almost brushed by me, then wheeled round again, and took up a position on the fence only a few yards from me. He was carrying what to him was an exceptionally large and heavy brick. He put it down beside him on the fence, and called out something which I could not understand. I did not move. He got quite excited and said some more. It was undoubtable he was addressing me—nobody else was by. I judged from his tone that he was getting cross with me. At this point my travelling companion, his toilet unfinished, put his head out of the window just above me.

"Such an odd thing," he called down to me. "I never noticed it last night. A pair of swallows are building a nest here in the hall. You've got to be careful you don't mistake it for a hat-peg. The old lady says they have built there regularly for the last three years."

Then it came to me what it was the gentleman had been saying to me: "I say, sir, you with the bit of wood in your mouth, you have been and shut the door and I can't get in."

Now, with the key in my possession, it was so clear and understandable, I really forgot for the moment he was only a bird.

"I beg your pardon," I replied, "I had no idea. Such an extraordinary place to build a nest."

I opened the door for him, and, taking up his brick again, he entered, and I followed him in. There was a deal of talk.

"He shut the door," I heard him say, "Chap there, sucking the bit of wood. Thought I was never going to get in."

"I know," was the answer; "it has been so dark in here, if you'll believe me, I've hardly been able to see what I've been doing."

"Fine brick, isn't it? Where will you have it?"

Observing me sitting there, they lowered their voices. Evidently she wanted him to put the brick down and leave her to think. She was not quite sure where she would have it. He, on the other hand, was sure he had found the right place for it. He pointed it out to her and explained his views. Other birds quarrel a good deal during nest building, but swallows are the gentlest of little people. She let him put it where he wanted to, and he kissed her and ran out. She cocked her eye after him, watched till he was out of sight, then deftly and quickly slipped it out and fixed it the other side of the door.

"Poor dears" (I could see it in the toss of her head); "they will think they know best; it is just as well not to argue with them."

Every summer I suffer much from indignation. I love to watch the swallows building. They build beneath the eaves outside my study window. Such cheerful little chatter-boxes they are. Long after sunset, when all the other birds are sleeping, the swallows still are chattering softly. It sounds as if they were telling one another some pretty story, and often I am sure there must be humour in it, for every now and then one hears a little twittering laugh. I delight in having them there, so close to me. The fancy comes to me that one day, when my brain has grown more cunning, I, too, listening in the twilight, shall hear the stories that they tell.

One or two phrases already I have come to understand: "Once upon a time"—"Long, long ago"—"In a strange, far-off land." I hear these words so constantly, I am sure I have them right. I call it "Swallow Street," this row of six or seven nests. Two or three, like villas in their own grounds, stand alone, and others are semi-detached. It makes me angry that the sparrows will come and steal them. The sparrows will hang about deliberately waiting for a pair of swallows to finish their nest, and then, with a brutal laugh that makes my blood boil, drive the swallows away and take possession of it. And the swallows are so wonderfully patient.

"Never mind, old girl," says Tommy Swallow, after the first big cry is over, to Jenny Swallow, "let's try again."

And half an hour later, full of fresh plans, they are choosing another likely site, chattering cheerfully once more. I watched the building of a particular nest for nearly a fortnight one year; and when, after two or three days' absence, I returned and found a pair of sparrows comfortably encsonced therein, I just felt mad. I saw Mrs. Sparrow looking out. Maybe my anger was working upon my imagination, but it seemed to me that she nodded to me:

"Nice little house, ain't it? What I call well built."

Mr. Sparrow then flew up with a gaudy feather, dyed blue, which belonged to me. I recognised it. It had come out of the brush with which the girl breaks the china ornaments in our drawing-room. At any other time I should have been glad to see him flying off with the whole thing, handle included. But now I felt the theft of that one feather as an added injury. Mrs. Sparrow chirped with delight at sight of the gaudy monstrosity. Having got the house cheap, they were going to spend their small amount of energy upon internal decoration. That was their idea clearly, a "Liberty interior." She looked more like a Cockney sparrow than a country one—had been born and bred in Regent Street, no doubt.

"There is not much justice in this world," said I to myself; "but there's going to be some introduced into this business—that is, if I can find a ladder."

I did find a ladder, and fortunately it was long enough. Mr. and Mrs. Sparrow were out when I arrived, possibly on the hunt for cheap photo frames and Japanese fans. I did not want to make a mess. I removed the house neatly into a dust-pan, and wiped the street clear of every trace of it. I had just put back the ladder when Mrs. Sparrow returned with a piece of pink cotton-wool in her mouth. That was her idea of a colour scheme: apple-blossom pink and Reckitt's blue side by side. She dropped her wool and sat on the waterspout, and tried to understand things.

"Number one, number two, number four; where the blazes"—sparrows are essentially common, and the women are as bad as the men—"is number three?"

Mr. Sparrow came up from behind, over the roof. He was carrying a piece of yellow-fluff, part of a lamp-shade, as far as I could judge.

"Move yourself," he said, "what's the sense of sitting there in the rain?"

"I went out just for a moment," replied Mrs. Sparrow; "I could not have been gone, no, not a couple of minutes. When I came back—"

"Oh, get indoors," said Mr. Sparrow, "talk about it there."

"It's what I'm telling you," continued Mrs. Sparrow, "if you would only listen. There isn't any door, there isn't any house—"

"Isn't any—" Mr. Sparrow, holding on to the rim of the spout, turned himself topsy-turvy and surveyed the street. From where I was standing behind the laurel bushes I could see nothing but his back.

He stood up again, looking angry and flushed.

"What have you done with the house? Can't I turn my back a minute—"

"I ain't done nothing with it. As I keep on telling you, I had only just gone—"

"Oh, bother where you had gone. Where's the darned house gone? that's what I want to know."

They looked at one another. If ever astonishment was expressed in the attitude of a bird it was told by the tails of those two sparrows. They whispered wickedly together. The idea occurred to them that by force or cunning they might perhaps obtain possession of one of the other nests. But all the other nests were occupied, and even gentle Jenny Swallow, once in her own home with the children round about her, is not to be trifled with. Mr. Sparrow called at number two, put his head in at the door, and then returned to the waterspout.

"Lady says we don't live there," he explained to Mrs. Sparrow. There was silence for a while.

"Not what I call a classy street," commented Mrs. Sparrow.

"If it were not for that terrible tired feeling of mine," said Mr. Sparrow, "blame if I wouldn't build a house of my own."

"Perhaps," said Mrs. Sparrow, "—I have heard it said that a little bit of work, now and then, does you good."

"All sorts of wild ideas about in the air nowadays," said Mr. Sparrow, "it don't do to listen to everybody."

"And it don't do to sit still and do nothing neither," snapped Mrs. Sparrow. "I don't want to have to forget I'm a lady, but—well, any man who was a man would see things for himself."

"Why did I every marry?" retorted Mr. Sparrow.

They flew away together, quarrelling.

DO WRITERS WRITE TOO MUCH?

On a newspaper placard, the other day, I saw announced a new novel by a celebrated author. I bought a copy of the paper, and turned eagerly to the last page. I was disappointed to find that I had missed the first six chapters. The story had commenced the previous Saturday; this was Friday. I say I was disappointed and so I was, at first. But my disappointment did not last long. The bright and intelligent sub-editor, according to the custom now in vogue, had provided me with a short synopsis of those first six chapters, so that without the trouble of reading them I knew what they were all about.

"The first instalment," I learned, "introduces the reader to a brilliant and distinguished company, assembled in the drawing-room of Lady Mary's maisonette in Park Street. Much smart talk is indulged in."

I know that "smart talk" so well. Had I not been lucky enough to miss that first chapter I should have had to listen to it once again. Possibly, here and there, it might have been new to me, but it would have read, I know, so very like the old. A dear, sweet white-haired lady of my acquaintance is never surprised at anything that happens.

"Something very much of the same kind occurred," she will remember, "one winter when we were staying in Brighton. Only on that occasion the man's name, I think, was Robinson."

We do not live new stories—nor write them either. The man's name in the old story was Robinson, we alter it to Jones. It happened, in the old forgotten tale, at Brighton, in the winter time; we change it to Eastbourne, in the spring. It is new and original—to those who have not heard "something very like it" once before.

"Much smart talk is indulged in," so the sub-editor has explained. There is absolutely no need to ask for more than that. There is a Duchess who says improper things. Once she used to shock me. But I know her now. She is really a nice woman; she doesn't mean them. And when the heroine is in trouble, towards the middle of the book, she is just as amusing on the side of virtue. Then there is a younger lady whose speciality is proverbs. Apparently whenever she hears a proverb she writes it down and studies it with the idea of seeing into how many different forms it can be twisted. It looks clever; as a matter of fact, it is extremely easy.

Be virtuous and you will be happy.

She jots down all the possible variations: Be virtuous and you will be unhappy.

"Too simple that one," she tells herself. Be virtuous and your friends will be happy if you are not.

"Better, but not wicked enough. Let us think again. Be happy and people will jump to the conclusion that you are virtuous.

"That's good, I'll try that one at to-morrow's party."

She is a painstaking lady. One feels that, better advised, she might have been of use in the world.

There is likewise a disgraceful old Peer who tells naughty stories, but who is good at heart; and one person so very rude that the wonder is who invited him.

Occasionally a slangy girl is included, and a clergyman, who takes the heroine aside and talks sense to her, flavoured with epigram. All these people chatter a mixture of Lord Chesterfield and Oliver Wendell Holmes, of Heine, Voltaire, Madame de Stael, and the late lamented H. J. Byron. "How they do it beats me," as I once overheard at a music hall a stout lady confess to her friend while witnessing the performance of a clever troup, styling themselves "The Boneless Wonders of the Universe."

The synopsis added that: "Ursula Bart, a charming and unsophisticated young American girl possessed of an elusive expression makes her first acquaintance with London society."

Here you have a week's unnecessary work on the part of the author boiled down to its essentials. She was young. One hardly expects an elderly heroine. The "young" might have been dispensed with, especially seeing it is told us that she was a girl. But maybe this is carping. There are young girls and old girls. Perhaps it is as well to have it in black and white; she was young. She was an American young girl. There is but one American young girl in English fiction. We know by heart the unconventional things that she will do, the startlingly original things that she will say, the fresh illuminating thoughts that will come to her as, clad in a loose robe of some soft clinging stuff, she sits before the fire, in the solitude of her own room.

To complete her she had an "elusive expression." The days when we used to catalogue the heroine's "points" are past. Formerly it was possible. A man wrote perhaps some half-a-dozen novels during the whole course of his career. He could have a dark girl for the first, a light girl for the second, sketch a merry little wench for the third, and draw you something stately for the fourth. For the remaining two he could go abroad. Nowadays, when a man turns out a novel and six short stories once a year, description has to be dispensed with. It is not the writer's fault. There is not sufficient variety in the sex. We used to introduce her thus:

"Imagine to yourself, dear reader, an exquisite and gracious creature of five feet three. Her golden hair of that peculiar shade"—here would follow directions enabling the reader to work it out for himself. He was to pour some particular wine into some particular sort of glass, and wave it about before some particular sort of a light. Or he was to get up at five o'clock on a March morning and go into a wood. In this way he could satisfy himself as to the particular shade of gold the heroine's hair might happen to be. If he were a careless or lazy reader he could save himself time and trouble by taking the author's word for it. Many of them did.

"Her eyes!" They were invariably deep and liquid. They had to be pretty deep to hold all the odds and ends that were hidden in them; sunlight and shadow, mischief, unsuspected possibilities, assorted emotions, strange wild yearnings. Anything we didn't know where else to put we said was hidden in her eyes.

"Her nose!" You could have made it for yourself out of a pen'orth of putty after reading our description of it.

"Her forehead!" It was always "low and broad." I don't know why it was always low. Maybe because the intellectual heroine was not then popular. For the matter of that I doubt if she be really popular now. The brainless doll, one fears, will continue for many years to come to be man's ideal woman—and woman's ideal of herself for precisely the same period, one may be sure.

"Her chin!" A less degree of variety was permissible in her chin. It had to be at an angle suggestive of piquancy, and it had to contain at least the suspicion of a dimple.

To properly understand her complexion you were expected to provide yourself with a collection of assorted fruits and flowers. There are seasons in the year when it must have been difficult for the conscientious reader to have made sure of her complexion. Possibly it was for this purpose that wax flowers and fruit, carefully kept from the dust under glass cases, were common objects in former times upon the tables of the cultured.

Nowadays we content ourselves—and our readers also, I am inclined to think—with dashing her off in a few bold strokes. We say that whenever she entered a room there came to one dreams of an old world garden, the sound of far-off bells. Or that her presence brought with it the scent of hollyhocks and thyme. As a matter of fact I don't think hollyhocks do smell. It is a small point; about such we do not trouble ourselves. In the case of the homely type of girl I don't see why we should not borrow Mr. Pickwick's expression, and define her by saying that in some subtle way she always contrived to suggest an odour of chops and tomato sauce.

If we desire to be exact we mention, as this particular author seems to have done, that she had an "elusive expression," or a penetrating fragrance. Or we say that she moved, the centre of an indefinable nuance.

But it is not policy to bind oneself too closely to detail. A wise friend of mine, who knows his business, describes his hero invariably in the vaguest terms. He will not even tell you whether the man is tall or short, clean shaven or bearded.

"Make the fellow nice," is his advice. "Let every woman reader picture him to herself as her particular man. Then everything he says and does becomes of importance to her. She is careful not to miss a word."

For the same reason he sees to it that his heroine has a bit of every girl in her. Generally speaking, she is a cross between Romola and Dora Copperfield. His novels command enormous sales. The women say he draws a man to the life, but does not seem to know much about women. The men like his women, but think his men stupid.

Of another famous author no woman of my acquaintance is able to speak too highly. They tell me his knowledge of their sex is simply marvellous, his insight, his understanding of them almost uncanny. Thinking it might prove useful, I made an exhaustive study of his books. I noticed that his women were without exception brilliant charming creatures possessed of the wit of a Lady Wortlay Montagu, combined with the wisdom of a George Eliot. They were not all of them good women, but all of them were clever and all of them were fascinating. I came to the conclusion that his lady critics were correct: he did understand women. But to return to our synopsis.

The second chapter, it appeared, transported us to Yorkshire where: "Basil Longleat, a typical young Englishman, lately home from college, resides with his widowed mother and two sisters. They are a delightful family."

What a world of trouble to both writer and to reader is here saved. "A typical young Englishman!" The author probably wrote five pages, elaborating. The five words of the sub-editor present him to me more vividly. I see him positively glistening from the effects of soap and water. I see his clear blue eye; his fair crisp locks, the natural curliness of which annoys him personally, though alluring to everybody else; his frank winning smile. He is "lately home from college." That tells me that he is a first-class cricketer; a first-class oar; that as a half-back he is incomparable; that he swims like Captain Webb; is in the first rank of tennis players; that his half-volley at ping-pong has never been stopped. It doesn't tell me much about his brain power. The description of him as a "typical young Englishman" suggests more information on this particular point. One assumes that the American girl with the elusive expression is going to have sufficient for both.

"They are a delightful family." The sub-editor does not say so, but I imagine the two sisters are likewise typical young Englishwomen. They ride and shoot and cook and make their own dresses, have common sense and love a joke.

The third chapter is "taken up with the humours of a local cricket match."

Thank you, Mr. Sub-editor. I feel I owe you gratitude.

In the fourth, Ursula Bart (I was beginning to get anxious about her) turns up again. She is staying at the useful Lady Mary's place in Yorkshire. She meets Basil by accident one morning while riding alone. That is the advantage of having an American girl for your heroine. Like the British army: it goes anywhere and does anything.

In chapter five Basil and Ursula meet again; this time at a picnic. The sub-editor does not wish to repeat himself, otherwise he possibly would have summed up chapter five by saying it was "taken up with the humours of the usual picnic."

In chapter six something happens:

"Basil, returning home in the twilight, comes across Ursula Bart, in a lonely point of the moor, talking earnestly to a rough-looking stranger. His approach over the soft turf being unnoticed, he cannot help overhearing Ursula's parting words to the forbidding-looking stranger: 'I must see you again! To-morrow night at half-past nine! In the gateway of the ruined abbey!' Who is he? And why must Ursula see him again at such an hour, in such a spot?"

So here, at cost of reading twenty lines, I am landed, so to speak, at the beginning of the seventh chapter. Why don't I set to work to read it? The sub-editor has spoiled me.

"You read it," I want to say to him. "Tell me to-morrow morning what it is all about. Who was this bounder? Why should Ursula want to see him again? Why choose a draughty place? Why half-past nine o'clock at night, which must have been an awkward time for both of them—likely to lead to talk? Why should I wade though this seventh chapter of three columns and a half? It's your work. What are you paid for?"

My fear is lest this sort of thing shall lead to a demand on the part of the public for condensed novels. What busy man is going to spend a week of evenings reading a book when a nice kind sub-editor is prepared in five minutes to tell him what it is all about!

Then there will come a day—I feel it—when the business-like Editor will say to himself: "What in thunder is the sense of my paying one man to write a story of sixty thousand words and another man to read it and tell it again in sixteen hundred!"

We shall be expected to write our novels in chapters not exceeding twenty words. Our short stories will be reduced to the formula: "Little boy. Pair of skates. Broken ice, Heaven's gates." Formerly an author, commissioned to supply a child's tragedy of this genre for a Christmas number, would have spun it out into five thousand words. Personally, I should have commenced the previous spring—given the reader the summer and autumn to get accustomed to the boy. He would have been a good boy; the sort of boy that makes a bee-line for the thinnest ice. He would have lived in a cottage. I could have spread that cottage over two pages; the things that grew in the garden, the view from the front door. You would have known that boy before I had done with him—felt you had known him all your life. His quaint sayings, his childish thoughts, his great longings would have been impressed upon you. The father might have had a dash of humour in him, the mother's early girlhood would have lent itself to pretty writing. For the ice we would have had a mysterious lake in the wood, said to be haunted. The boy would have loved o' twilights to stand upon its margin. He would have heard strange voices calling to him. You would have felt the thing was coming.

So much might have been done. When I think of that plot wasted in nine words it makes me positively angry.

48

And what is to become of us writers if this is to be the new fashion in literature? We are paid by the length of our manuscript at rates from half-a-crown a thousand words, and upwards. In the case of fellows like Doyle and Kipling I am told it runs into pounds. How are we to live on novels the serial rights of which to most of us will work out at four and nine-pence.

It can't be done. It is no good telling me you can see no reason why we should live. That is no answer. I'm talking plain business.

And what about book-rights? Who is going to buy novels of three pages? They will have to be printed as leaflets and sold at a penny a dozen. Marie Corelli and Hall Caine—if all I hear about them is true— will possibly make their ten or twelve shillings a week. But what about the rest of us? This thing is worrying me.

SHOULD SOLDIERS BE POLITE?

My desire was once to pass a peaceful and pleasant winter in Brussels, attending to my work, improving my mind. Brussels is a bright and cheerful town, and I think I could have succeeded had it not been for the Belgian Army. The Belgian Army would follow me about and worry me. Judging of it from my own experience, I should say it was a good army. Napoleon laid it down as an axiom that your enemy never ought to be permitted to get away from you—never ought to be allowed to feel, even for a moment, that he had shaken you off. What tactics the Belgian Army might adopt under other conditions I am unable to say, but against me personally that was the plan of campaign it determined upon and carried out with a success that was astonishing, even to myself.

I found it utterly impossible to escape from the Belgian Army. I made a point of choosing the quietest and most unlikely streets, I chose all hours—early in the morning, in the afternoon, late in the evening. There were moments of wild exaltation when I imagined I had given it the slip. I could not see it anywhere, I could not hear it.

"Now," said I to myself, "now for five minutes' peace and quiet."

I had been doing it injustice: it had been working round me. Approaching the next corner, I would hear the tattoo of its drum. Before I had gone another quarter of a mile it would be in full pursuit of me. I would jump upon a tram, and travel for miles. Then, thinking I had shaken it off, I would alight and proceed upon my walk. Five minutes later another detachment would be upon my heels. I would slink home, the Belgian Army pursuing me with its exultant tattoo. Vanquished, shamed, my insular pride for ever vanished, I would creep up into my room and close the door. The victorious Belgian Army would then march back to barracks.

If only it had followed me with a band: I like a band. I can loaf against a post, listening to a band with anyone. I should not have minded so much had it come after me with a band. But the Belgian Army, apparently, doesn't run to a band. It has nothing but this drum. It has not even a real drum—not what I call a drum. It is a little boy's drum, the sort of thing I used to play myself at one time, until people took it away from me, and threatened that if they heard it once again that day they would break it over my own head. It is cowardly going up and down, playing a drum of this sort, when there is nobody to stop you. The man would not dare to do it if his mother was about. He does not even play it. He walks along tapping it with a little stick. There's no tune, there's no sense in it. He does not even keep time. I used to think at first, hearing it in the distance, that it was the work of some young gamin who ought to be at school, or making himself useful taking the baby out in the perambulator: and I would draw back into dark doorways, determined, as he came by, to dart out and pull his ear for him. To my astonishment—for the first week—I learnt it was the Belgian Army, getting itself accustomed, one supposes, to the horrors of war. It had the effect of making me a peace-at-any-price man.

They tell me these armies are necessary to preserve the tranquility of Europe. For myself, I should be willing to run the risk of an occasional row. Cannot someone tell them they are out of date, with their bits of feathers and their odds and ends of ironmongery—grown men that cannot be sent out for a walk unless accompanied by a couple of nursemen, blowing a tin whistle and tapping a drum out of a toy shop to keep them in order and prevent their running about: one might think they were chickens. A herd of soldiers with their pots and pans and parcels, and all their deadly things tied on to them, prancing about in time to a tune, makes me think always of the White Knight that Alice met in Wonderland. I take it that for practical purposes—to fight for your country, or to fight for somebody else's country, which is, generally speaking, more popular—the thing essential is that a certain proportion of the populace should be able to shoot straight with a gun. How standing in a line and turning out your toes is going to assist you, under modern conditions of warfare, is one of the many things my intellect is incapable of grasping.

In mediaeval days, when men fought hand to hand, there must have been advantage in combined and precise movement. When armies were mere iron machines, the simple endeavour of each being to push the other off the earth, then the striking simultaneously with a thousand arms was part of the game. Now, when we shoot from behind cover with smokeless powder, brain not brute force—individual sense not combined solidity is surely the result to be aimed at. Cannot somebody, as I have suggested, explain to the military man that the proper place for the drill sergeant nowadays is under a glass case in some museum of antiquities?

I lived once near the Hyde Park barracks, and saw much of the drill sergeant's method. Generally speaking, he is a stout man with the walk of an egotistical pigeon. His voice is one of the most extraordinary things in nature: if you can distinguish it from the bark of a dog, you are clever. They tell me that the privates, after a little practice, can—which gives one a higher opinion of their intelligence than otherwise one might form. But myself I doubt even this statement. I was the owner of a fine retriever dog about the time of which I am speaking, and sometimes he and I would amuse ourselves by watching Mr. Sergeant exercising his squad. One morning he had been shouting out the usual "Whough, whough, whough!" for about ten minutes, and all had hitherto gone well. Suddenly, and evidently to his intense astonishment, the squad turned their backs upon him and commenced to walk towards the Serpentine.

"Halt!" yelled the sergeant, the instant his amazed indignation permitted him to speak, which fortunately happened in time to save the detachment from a watery grave.

The squad halted.

"Who the thunder, and the blazes, and other things told you to do that?"

The squad looked bewildered, but said nothing, and were brought back to the place where they were before. A minute later precisely the same thing occurred again. I really thought the sergeant would burst. I was preparing to hasten to the barracks for medical aid. But the paroxysm passed. Calling upon the combined forces of heaven and hell to sustain him in his trouble, he requested his squad, as man to man, to inform him of the reason why to all appearance they were dispensing with his services and drilling themselves.

At this moment "Columbus" barked again, and the explanation came to him.

"Please go away, sir," he requested me. "How can I exercise my men with that dog of yours interfering every five minutes?"

It was not only on that occasion. It happened at other times. The dog seemed to understand and take a pleasure in it. Sometimes meeting a soldier, walking with his sweetheart, Columbus, from behind my legs, would bark suddenly. Immediately the man would let go the girl and proceed, involuntarily, to perform military tricks.

The War Office authorities accused me of having trained the dog. I had not trained him: that was his natural voice. I suggested to the War Office authorities that instead of quarrelling with my dog for talking his own language, they should train their sergeants to use English.

They would not see it. Unpleasantness was in the air, and, living where I did at the time, I thought it best to part with Columbus. I could see what the War Office was driving at, and I did not desire that responsibility for the inefficiency of the British Army should be laid at my door.

Some twenty years ago we, in London, were passing through a riotous period, and a call was made to law-abiding citizens to enrol themselves as special constables. I was young, and the hope of trouble appealed to me more than it does now. In company with some five or six hundred other more or less respectable citizens, I found myself one Sunday morning in the drill yard of the Albany Barracks. It was the opinion of the authorities that we could guard our homes and protect our wives and children better if first of all we learned to roll our "eyes right" or left at the given word of command, and to walk with our thumbs stuck out. Accordingly a drill sergeant was appointed to instruct us on these points. He came out of the canteen, wiping his mouth and flicking his leg, according to rule, with the regulation cane. But, as he approached us, his expression changed. We were stout, pompous-looking gentlemen, the majority of us, in frock coats and silk hats. The sergeant was a man with a sense of the fitness of things. The idea of shouting and swearing at us fell from him: and that gone there seemed to be no happy medium left to him. The stiffness departed from his back. He met us with a defferential attitude, and spoke to us in the language of social intercourse.

"Good morning, gentlemen," said the sergeant.

"Good morning," we replied: and there was a pause.

The sergeant fidgetted upon his feet. We waited.

"Well, now, gentlemen," said the sergeant, with a pleasant smile, "what do you say to falling in?"

We agreed to fall in. He showed us how to do it. He cast a critical eye along the back of our rear line.

"A little further forward, number three, if you don't mind, sir," he suggested.

Number three, who was an important-looking gentleman, stepped forward.

The sergeant cast his critical eye along the front of the first line.

"A little further back, if you don't mind, sir," he suggested, addressing the third gentleman from the end.

"Can't," explained the third gentleman, "much as I can do to keep where I am."

The sergeant cast his critical eye between the lines.

"Ah," said the sergeant, "a little full-chested, some of us. We will make the distance another foot, if you please, gentlemen."

In pleasant manner, like to this, the drill proceeded.

"Now then, gentlemen, shall we try a little walk? Quick march! Thank you, gentlemen. Sorry to trouble you, but it may be necessary to run—forward I mean, of course.. So if you really do not mind, we will now do the double quick. Halt! And if next time you can keep a little more in line—it has a more imposing appearance, if you understand me. The breathing comes with practice."

If the thing must be done at all, why should it not be done in this way? Why should not the sergeant address the new recruits politely:

"Now then, you young chaps, are you all ready? Don't hurry yourselves: no need to make hard work of what should be a pleasure to all of us. That's right, that's very good indeed—considering you are only novices. But there is still something to be desired in your attitude, Private Bully-boy. You will excuse my being personal, but are you knock-kneed naturally? Or could you, with an effort, do you think, contrive to give yourself less the appearance of a marionette whose strings have become loose? Thank you, that is better. These little things appear trivial, I know, but, after all, we may as well try and look our best—

"Don't you like your boots, Private Montmorency? Oh, I beg your pardon. I thought from the way you were bending down and looking at them that perhaps their appearance was dissatisfying to you. My mistake.

"Are you suffering from indigestion, my poor fellow? Shall I get you a little brandy? It isn't indigestion. Then what's the matter with it? Why are you trying to hide it? It's nothing to be ashamed of. We've all got one. Let it come forward man. Let's see it."

Having succeeded, with a few such kindly words, in getting his line into order, he would proceed to recommend healthy exercise.

"Shoulder arms! Good, gentlemen, very good for a beginning. Yet still, if I may be critical, not perfect. There is more in this thing than you might imagine, gentlemen. May I point out to Private Henry Thompson that a musket carried across the shoulder at right angles is apt to inconvenience the gentleman behind. Even from the point of view of his own comfort, I feel sure that Private Thompson would do better to follow the usual custom in this matter.

"I would also suggest to Private St. Leonard that we are not here to practice the art of balancing a heavy musket on the outstretched palm of the hand. Private St. Leonard's performance with the musket is decidedly clever. But it is not war.

"Believe me, gentlemen, this thing has been carefully worked out, and no improvement is likely to result from individual effort. Let our idea be uniformity. It is monotonous, but it is safe. Now, then, gentlemen, once again."

The drill yard would be converted into a source of innocent delight to thousands. "Officer and gentleman" would become a phrase of meaning. I present the idea, for what it may be worth, with my compliments, to Pall Mall.

The fault of the military man is that he studies too much, reads too much history, is over reflective. If, instead, he would look about him more he would notice that things are changing. Someone has told the British military man that Waterloo was won upon the playing fields of Eton. So he goes to Eton and plays. One of these days he will be called upon to fight another Waterloo: and afterwards—when it is too late—they will explain to him that it was won not upon the play field but in the class room.

From the mound on the old Waterloo plain one can form a notion of what battles, under former conditions, must have been. The other battlefields of Europe are rapidly disappearing: useful Dutch cabbages, as Carlyle would have pointed out with justifiable satisfaction, hiding the theatre of man's childish folly. You find, generally speaking, cobblers happily employed in cobbling shoes, women gossiping cheerfully over the washtub on the spot where a hundred years ago, according to the guide-book, a thousand men dressed in blue and a thousand men dressed in red rushed together like quarrelsome fox-terriers, and worried each other to death.

But the field of Waterloo is little changed. The guide, whose grandfather was present at the battle—quite an extraordinary number of grandfathers must have fought at Waterloo: there must have been whole regiments composed of grandfathers—can point out to you the ground across which every charge was delivered, can show you every ridge, still existing, behind which the infantry crouched. The whole business was began and finished within a space little larger than a square mile. One can understand the advantage then to be derived from the perfect moving of the military machine; the uses of the echelon, the purposes of the linked battalion, the manipulation of centre, left wing and right wing. Then it may have been worth while—if war be ever worth the while—which grown men of sense are beginning to doubt—to waste two years of a soldier's training, teaching him the goose-step. In the twentieth century, teaching soldiers the evolutions of the Thirty Years' War is about as sensible as it would be loading our iron-clads with canvas.

I followed once a company of Volunteers across Blackfriars Bridge on their way from Southwark to the Temple. At the bottom of Ludgate Hill the commanding officer, a young but conscientious gentleman, ordered "Left wheel!" At once the vanguard turned down a narrow alley—I forget its name—which would have led the troop into the purlieus of Whitefriars, where, in all probability, they would have been lost for ever. The whole company had to be halted, right-about-faced, and retired a hundred yards. Then the order "Quick march!" was given. The vanguard shot across Ludgate Circus, and were making for the Meat Market.

At this point that young commanding officer gave up being a military man and talked sense.

"Not that way," he shouted: "up Fleet Street and through Middle Temple Lane."

Then without further trouble the army of the future went upon its way.

OUGHT STORIES TO BE TRUE?

There was once upon a time a charming young lady, possessed of much taste, who was asked by her anxious parent, the years passing and family expenditure not decreasing, which of the numerous and eligible young men then paying court to her she liked the best. She replied, that was her difficulty; she could not make up her mind which she liked the best. They were all so nice. She could not possibly select one to the exclusion of all the others. What she would have liked would have been to marry the lot; but that, she presumed, was impracticable.

I feel I resemble that young lady, not so much in charm and beauty as in indecision of mind, when the question is that of my favourite author or my favourite book. It is as if one were asked one's favourite food. There are times when one fancies an egg with one's tea. On other occasions one dreams of a kipper. To-day one clamours for lobsters. To-morrow one feels one never wishes to see a lobster again. One determines to settle down, for a time, to a diet of bread and milk and rice pudding. Asked suddenly to say whether I preferred ices to soup, or beef-steak to caviare, I should be completely nonplussed.

There may be readers who care for only one literary diet. I am a person of gross appetites, requiring many authors to satisfy me. There are moods when the savage strength of the Bronte sisters is companionable to me. One rejoices in the unrelieved gloom of "Wuthering Heights," as in the lowering skies of a stormy autumn. Perhaps part of the marvel of the book comes from the knowledge that the authoress was a slight, delicate young girl. One wonders what her future work would have been, had she lived to gain a wider experience of life; or was it well for her fame that nature took the pen so soon from her hand? Her suppressed vehemence may have been better suited to those tangled Yorkshire by-ways than to the more open, cultivated fields of life.

There is not much similarity between the two books, yet when recalling Emily Bronte my thoughts always run on to Olive Schreiner. Here, again, was a young girl with the voice of a strong man. Olive Schreiner, more fortunate, has lived; but I doubt if she will ever write a book that will remind us of her first. "The Story of an African Farm" is not a work to be repeated. We have advanced in literature of late. I can well remember the storm of indignation with which the "African Farm" was received by Mrs. Grundy and her then numerous, but now happily diminishing, school. It was a book that was to be kept from the hands of every young man and woman. But the hands of the young men and women stretched out and grasped it, to their help. It is a curious idea, this of Mrs. Grundy's, that the young man and woman must never think—that all literature that does anything more than echo the conventions must be hidden away.

Then there are times when I love to gallop through history on Sir Walter's broomstick. At other hours it is pleasant to sit in converse with wise George Eliot. From her garden terrace I look down on Loamshire and its commonplace people; while in her quiet, deep voice she tells me of the hidden hearts that beat and throb beneath these velveteen jackets and lace falls.

Who can help loving Thackeray, wittiest, gentlest of men, in spite of the faint suspicion of snobbishness that clings to him? There is something pathetic in the good man's horror of this snobbishness, to which he himself was a victim. May it not have been an affectation, born unconsciously of self-consciousness? His heroes and heroines must needs be all fine folk, fit company for lady and gentlemen readers. To him the livery was too often the man. Under his stuffed calves even Jeames de la Pluche himself stood upon the legs of a man, but Thackeray could never see deeper than the silk stockings. Thackeray lived and died in Clubland. One feels that the world was bounded for him by Temple Bar on the east and Park Lane on the west; but what there was good in Clubland he showed us, and for the sake of the great gentlemen and sweet ladies that his kindly eyes found in that narrow region, not too overpeopled with great gentlemen and sweet women, let us honour him.

"Tom Jones," "Peregrine Pickle," and "Tristram Shandy" are books a man is the better for reading, if he read them wisely. They teach him that literature, to be a living force, must deal with all sides of life, and that little help comes to us from that silly pretence of ours that we are perfect in all things, leading perfect lives, that only the villain of the story ever deviates from the path of rectitude.

This is a point that needs to be considered by both the makers and the buyers of stories. If literature is to be regarded solely as the amusement of an idle hour, then the less relationship it has to life the better. Looking into a truthful mirror of nature we are compelled to think; and when thought comes in at the window self-satisfaction goes out by the door. Should a novel or play call us to ponder upon the problems of existence, or lure us from the dusty high road of the world, for a while, into the pleasant meadows of dreamland? If only the latter, then let our heroes and our heroines be not what men and women are, but what they should be. Let Angelina be always spotless and Edwin always true. Let virtue ever triumph over villainy in the last chapter; and let us assume that the marriage service answers all the questions of the Sphinx.

Very pleasant are these fairy tales where the prince is always brave and handsome; where the princess is always the best and most beautiful princess that ever lived; where one knows the wicked people at a glance by their ugliness and ill-temper, mistakes being thus rendered impossible; where the good fairies are, by nature, more powerful than the bad; where gloomy paths lead ever to fair palaces; where the dragon is ever vanquished; and where well-behaved husbands and wives can rely upon living happily ever afterwards. "The world is too much with us, late and soon." It is wise to slip away from it at times to fairyland. But, alas, we cannot live in fairyland, and knowledge of its geography is of little help to us on our return to the rugged country of reality.

Are not both branches of literature needful? By all means let us dream, on midsummer nights, of fond lovers led through devious paths to happiness by Puck; of virtuous dukes—one finds such in fairyland; of fate subdued by faith and gentleness. But may we not also, in our more serious humours, find satisfaction in thinking with Hamlet or Coriolanus? May not both Dickens and Zola have their booths in Vanity Fair? If literature is to be a help to us, as well as a pastime, it must deal with the ugly as well as with the beautiful; it must show us ourselves, not as we wish to appear, but as we know ourselves to be. Man has been described as a animal with aspirations reaching up to Heaven and instincts rooted—elsewhere. Is literature to flatter him, or reveal him to himself?

Of living writers it is not safe, I suppose, to speak except, perhaps, of those who have been with us so long that we have come to forget they are not of the past. Has justice ever been done to Ouida's undoubted genius by our shallow school of criticism, always very clever in discovering faults as obvious as pimples on a fine face? Her guardsmen "toy" with their food. Her horses win the Derby three years running. Her wicked women throw guinea peaches from the windows of the Star and Garter into the Thames at Richmond. The distance being about three hundred and fifty yards, it is a good throw. Well, well, books are not made worth reading by the absence of absurdities. Ouida possesses strength, tenderness, truth, passion; and these be qualities in a writer capable of carrying many more faults than Ouida is burdened with. But that is the method of our little criticism. It views an artist as Gulliver saw the Brobdingnag ladies. It is too small to see them in their entirety: a mole or a wart absorbs all its vision.

Why was not George Gissing more widely read? If faithfulness to life were the key to literary success, Gissing's sales would have been counted by the million instead of by the hundred.

Have Mark Twain's literary qualities, apart altogether from his humour, been recognised in literary circles as they ought to have been? "Huck Finn" would be a great work were there not a laugh in it from cover to cover. Among the Indians and some other savage tribes the fact that a member of the community has lost one of his senses makes greatly to his advantage; he is then regarded as a superior person. So among a school of Anglo-Saxon readers, it is necessary to a man, if he would gain literary credit, that he should lack the sense of humour. One or two curious modern examples occur to me of literary success secured chiefly by this failing.

All these authors are my favourites; but such catholic taste is held nowadays to be no taste. One is told that if one loves Shakespeare, one must of necessity hate Ibsen; that one cannot appreciate Wagner and tolerate Beethoven; that if we admit any merit in Dore, we are incapable of understanding Whistler. How can I say which is my favourite novel? I can only ask myself which lives clearest in my memory, which is the book I run to more often than to another in that pleasant half hour before the dinner-bell, when, with all apologies to good Mr. Smiles, it is useless to think of work.

I find, on examination, that my "David Copperfield" is more dilapidated than any other novel upon my shelves. As I turn its dog-eared pages, reading the familiar headlines "Mr. Micawber in difficulties," "Mr. Micawber in prison," "I fall in love with Dora," "Mr. Barkis goes out with the tide," "My child wife," "Traddles in a nest of roses"—pages of my own life recur to me; so many of my sorrows, so many of my joys are woven in my mind with this chapter or the other. That day—how well I remember it when I read of "David's" wooing, but Dora's death

I was careful to skip. Poor, pretty little Mrs. Copperfield at the gate, holding up her baby in her arms, is always associated in my memory with a child's cry, long listened for. I found the book, face downwards on a chair, weeks afterwards, not moved from where I had hastily laid it.

Old friends, all of you, how many times have I not slipped away from my worries into your pleasant company! Peggotty, you dear soul, the sight of your kind eyes is so good to me. Our mutual friend, Mr. Charles Dickens, is prone, we know, just ever so slightly to gush. Good fellow that he is, he can see no flaw in those he loves, but you, dear lady, if you will permit me to call you by a name much abused, he has drawn in true colours. I know you well, with your big heart, your quick temper, your homely, human ways of thought. You yourself will never guess your worth—how much the world is better for such as you! You think of yourself as of a commonplace person, useful only for the making of pastry, the darning of stockings, and if a man—not a young man, with only dim half-opened eyes, but a man whom life had made keen to see the beauty that lies hidden beneath plain faces—were to kneel and kiss your red, coarse hand, you would be much astonished. But he would be a wise man, Peggotty, knowing what things a man should take carelessly, and for what things he should thank God, who has fashioned fairness in many forms.

Mr. Wilkins Micawber, and you, most excellent of faithful wives, Mrs. Emma Micawber, to you I also raise my hat. How often has the example of your philosophy saved me, when I, likewise, have suffered under the temporary pressure of pecuniary liabilities; when the sun of my prosperity, too, has sunk beneath the dark horizon of the world—in short, when I, also, have found myself in a tight corner. I have asked myself what would the Micawbers have done in my place. And I have answered myself. They would have sat down to a dish of lamb's fry, cooked and breaded by the deft hands of Emma, followed by a brew of punch, concocted by the beaming Wilkins, and have forgotten all their troubles, for the time being. Whereupon, seeing first that sufficient small change was in my pocket, I have entered the nearest restaurant, and have treated myself to a repast of such sumptuousness as the aforesaid small change would command, emerging from that restaurant stronger and more fit for battle. And lo! the sun of my prosperity has peeped at me from over the clouds with a sly wink, as if to say "Cheer up; I am only round the corner."

Cheery, elastic Mr. and Mrs. Micawber, how would half the world face their fate but by the help of a kindly, shallow nature such as yours? I love to think that your sorrows can be drowned in nothing more harmful than a bowl of punch. Here's to you, Emma, and to you, Wilkins, and to the twins!

May you and such childlike folk trip lightly over the stones upon your path! May something ever turn up for you, my dears! May the rain of life ever fall as April showers upon your simple bald head, Micawber!

And you, sweet Dora, let me confess I love you, though sensible friends deem you foolish. Ah, silly Dora, fashioned by wise Mother Nature who knows that weakness and helplessness are as a talisman calling forth strength and tenderness in man, trouble yourself not unduly about the oysters and the underdone mutton, little woman. Good plain cooks at twenty pounds a year will see to these things for us. Your work is to teach us gentleness and kindness. Lay your foolish curls just here, child. It is from such as you we learn wisdom. Foolish wise folk sneer at you. Foolish wise folk would pull up the laughing lilies, the needless roses from the garden, would plant in their places only useful, wholesome cabbage. But the gardener, knowing better, plants the silly, short-lived flowers, foolish wise folk asking for what purpose.

Gallant Traddles, of the strong heart and the unruly hair; Sophy, dearest of girls; Betsy Trotwood, with your gentlemanly manners and your woman's heart, you have come to me in shabby rooms, making the dismal place seem bright. In dark hours your kindly faces have looked out at me from the shadows, your kindly voices have cheered me.

Little Em'ly and Agnes, it may be my bad taste, but I cannot share my friend Dickens' enthusiasm for them. Dickens' good women are all too good for human nature's daily food. Esther Summerson, Florence Dombey, Little Nell—you have no faults to love you by.

Scott's women were likewise mere illuminated texts. Scott only drew one live heroine—Catherine Seton. His other women were merely the prizes the hero had to win in the end, like the sucking pig or the leg of mutton for which the yokel climbs the greasy pole. That Dickens could draw a woman to some likeness he proved by Bella Wilfer, and Estella in "Great Expectations." But real women have never been popular in fiction. Men readers prefer the false, and women readers object to the truth.

From an artistic point of view, "David Copperfield" is undoubtedly Dickens' best work. Its humour is less boisterous; its pathos less highly coloured.

One of Leech's pictures represents a cab-man calmly sleeping in the gutter.

"Oh, poor dear, he's ill," says a tender-hearted lady in the crowd. "Ill!" retorts a male bystander indignantly, "Ill! 'E's 'ad too much of what I ain't 'ad enough of."

Dickens suffered from too little of what some of us have too much of—criticism. His work met with too little resistance to call forth his powers. Too often his pathos sinks to bathos, and this not from want of skill, but from want of care. It is difficult to believe that the popular writer who allowed his sentimentality—or rather the public's sentimentality—to run away with him in such scenes as the death of Paul Dombey and Little Nell was the artist who painted the death of Sidney Carton and of Barkis, the willing. The death of Barkis, next to the passing of Colonel Newcome, is, to my thinking, one of the most perfect pieces of pathos in English literature. No very deep emotion is concerned. He is a commonplace old man, clinging foolishly to a commonplace box. His simple wife and the old boatmen stand by, waiting calmly for the end. There is no straining after effect. One feels death enter, dignifying all things; and touched by that hand, foolish old Barkis grows great.

In Uriah Heap and Mrs. Gummidge, Dickens draws types rather than characters. Pecksniff, Podsnap, Dolly Varden, Mr. Bumble, Mrs. Gamp, Mark Tapley, Turveydrop, Mrs. Jellyby—these are not characters; they are human characteristics personified.

We have to go back to Shakespeare to find a writer who, through fiction, has so enriched the thought of the people. Admit all Dickens' faults twice over, we still have one of the greatest writers of modern times. Such people as these creations of Dickens never lived, says your little critic. Nor was Prometheus, type of the spirit of man, nor was Niobe, mother of all mothers, a truthful picture of the citizen one was likely to meet often during a morning's stroll through Athens. Nor grew there ever a wood like to the Forest of Arden, though every Rosalind and Orlando knows the path to glades having much resemblance thereto.

Steerforth, upon whom Dickens evidently prided himself, I must confess, never laid hold of me. He is a melodramatic young man. The worst I could have wished him would have been that he should marry Rose Dartle and live with his mother. It would have served him right for being so attractive. Old Peggotty and Ham are, of course, impossible. One must accept them also as types. These Brothers Cheeryble, these Kits, Joe Gargeries, Boffins, Garlands, John Peerybingles, we will accept as types of the goodness that is in men—though in real life the amount of virtue that Dickens often wastes upon a single individual would by more economically minded nature, be made to serve for fifty.

To sum up, "David Copperfield" is a plain tale, simply told; and such are all books that live. Eccentricities of style, artistic trickery, may please the critic of a day, but literature is a story that interests us, boys and girls, men and women. It is a sad book; and that, again, gives it an added charm in these sad later days. Humanity is nearing its old age, and we have come to love sadness, as the friend who has been longest with us. In the young days of our vigour we were merry. With Ulysses' boatmen, we took alike the sunshine and the thunder with frolic welcome. The red blood flowed in our veins, and we laughed, and our tales were of strength and hope. Now we sit like old men, watching faces in the fire; and the stories that we love are sad stories—like the stories we ourselves have lived.

CREATURES THAT ONE DAY SHALL BE MEN.

I ought to like Russia better than I do, if only for the sake of the many good friends I am proud to possess amongst the Russians. A large square photograph I keep always on my mantel-piece; it helps me to maintain my head at that degree of distention necessary for the performance of all literary work. It presents in the centre a neatly-written address in excellent English that I frankly confess I am never tired of reading, around which are ranged some hundreds of names I am quite unable to read, but which, in spite of their strange lettering, I know to be the names of good Russian men and women to whom, a year or two ago, occurred the kindly idea of sending me as a Christmas card this message of encouragement. The individual Russian is one of the most charming creatures living. If he like you he does not hesitate to let you know it; not only by every action possible, but, by what perhaps is just as useful in this grey old world, by generous, impulsive speech.

We Anglo-Saxons are apt to pride ourselves upon being undemonstrative. Max Adeler tells the tale of a boy who was sent out by his father to fetch wood. The boy took the opportunity of disappearing and did not show his face again beneath the paternal roof for over twenty years. Then one evening, a smiling, well-dressed stranger entered to the old couple, and announced himself as their long-lost child, returned at last.

"Well, you haven't hurried yourself," grumbled the old man, "and blarm me if now you haven't forgotten the wood."

I was lunching with an Englishman in a London restaurant one day. A man entered and took his seat at a table near by. Glancing round, and meeting my friend's eyes, he smiled and nodded.

"Excuse me a minute," said my friend, "I must just speak to my brother—haven't seen him for over five years."

He finished his soup and leisurely wiped his moustache before strolling across and shaking hands. They talked for a while. Then my friend returned to me.

"Never thought to see him again," observed my friend, "he was one of the garrison of that place in Africa—what's the name of it?—that the Mahdi attacked. Only three of them escaped. Always was a lucky beggar, Jim."

"But wouldn't you like to talk to him some more?" I suggested; "I can see you any time about this little business of ours."

"Oh, that's all right," he answered, "we have just fixed it up—shall be seeing him again to-morrow."

I thought of this scene one evening while dining with some Russian friends in a St. Petersburg Hotel. One of the party had not seen his second cousin, a mining engineer, for nearly eighteen months. They sat opposite to one another, and a dozen times at least during the course of the dinner one of them would jump up from his chair, and run round to embrace the other. They would throw their arms about one another, kissing one another on both cheeks, and then sit down again, with moist eyes. Their behaviour among their fellow countrymen excited no astonishment whatever.

But the Russians's anger is as quick and vehement as his love. On another occasion I was supping with friends in one of the chief restaurants on the Nevsky. Two gentlemen at an adjoining table, who up till the previous moment had been engaged in amicable conversation, suddenly sprang to their feet, and "went for" one another. One man secured the water-bottle, which he promptly broke over the other's head. His opponent chose for his weapon a heavy mahogany chair, and leaping back for the purpose of securing a good swing, lurched against my hostess.

"Do please be careful," said the lady.

"A thousand pardons, madame," returned the stranger, from whom blood and water were streaming in equal copiousness; and taking the utmost care to avoid interfering with our comfort, he succeeded adroitly in flooring his antagonist by a well-directed blow.

A policeman appeared upon the scene. He did not attempt to interfere, but running out into the street communicated the glad tidings to another policeman.

"This is going to cost them a pretty penny," observed my host, who was calmly continuing his supper; "why couldn't they wait?"

It did cost them a pretty penny. Some half a dozen policemen were round about before as many minutes had elapsed, and each one claimed his bribe. Then they wished both combatants good-night, and trooped out evidently in great good humour and the two gentlemen, with wet napkins round their heads, sat down again, and laughter and amicable conversation flowed freely as before.

They strike the stranger as a childlike people, but you are possessed with a haunting sense of ugly traits beneath. The workers—slaves it would be almost more correct to call them—allow themselves to be exploited with the uncomplaining patience of intelligent animals. Yet every educated Russian you talk to on the subject knows that revolution is coming.

But he talks to you about it with the door shut, for no man in Russia can be sure that his own servants are not police spies. I was discussing politics with a Russian official one evening in his study when his old housekeeper entered the room—a soft-eyed grey-haired woman who had been in his service over eight years, and whose position in the household was almost that of a friend. He stopped abruptly and changed the conversation. So soon as the door was closed behind her again, he explained himself.

"It is better to chat upon such matters when one is quite alone," he laughed.

"But surely you can trust her," I said, "She appears to be devoted to you all."

"It is safer to trust no one," he answered. And then he continued from the point where we had been interrupted.

"It is gathering," he said; "there are times when I almost smell blood in the air. I am an old man and may escape it, but my children will have to suffer—suffer as children must for the sins of their fathers. We have made brute beasts of the people, and as brute beasts they will come upon us, cruel, and undiscriminating; right and wrong indifferently going down before them. But it has to be. It is needed."

It is a mistake to speak of the Russian classes opposing to all progress a dead wall of selfishness. The history of Russia will be the history of the French Revolution over again, but with this difference: that the educated classes, the thinkers, who are pushing forward the dumb masses are doing so with their eyes open. There will be no Maribeau, no Danton to be appalled at a people's ingratitude. The men who are to-day working for revolution in Russia number among their ranks statesmen, soldiers, delicately-nurtured women, rich landowners, prosperous tradesmen, students familiar with the lessons of history. They have no misconceptions concerning the blind Monster into which they are breathing life. He will crush them, they know it; but with them he will crush the injustice and stupidity they have grown to hate more than they love themselves.

The Russian peasant, when he rises, will prove more terrible, more pitiless than were the men of 1790. He is less intelligent, more brutal. They sing a wild, sad song, these Russian cattle, the while they work. They sing it in chorus on the quays while hauling the cargo, they sing it in the factory, they chant on the weary, endless steppes, reaping the corn they may not eat. It is of the good time their masters are having, of the feastings and the merrymakings, of the laughter of the children, of the kisses of the lovers.

But the last line of every verse is the same. When you ask a Russian to translate it for you he shrugs his shoulders.

"Oh, it means," he says, "that their time will also come—some day."

It is a pathetic, haunting refrain. They sing it in the drawing-rooms of Moscow and St. Petersburg, and somehow the light talk and laughter die away, and a hush, like a chill breath, enters by the closed door and passes through. It is a curious song, like the wailing of a tired wind, and one day it will sweep over the land heralding terror.

A Scotsman I met in Russia told me that when he first came out to act as manager of a large factory in St. Petersburg, belonging to his Scottish employers, he unwittingly made a mistake the first week when paying his workpeople. By a miscalculation of the Russian money he paid the men, each one, nearly a rouble short. He discovered his error before the following Saturday, and then put the matter right. The men accepted his explanation with perfect composure and without any comment whatever. The thing astonished him.

"But you must have known I was paying you short," he said to one of them. "Why didn't you tell me of it?"

"Oh," answered the man, "we thought you were putting it in your own pocket and then if we had complained it would have meant dismissal for us. No one would have taken our word against yours."

Corruption appears to be so general throughout the whole of Russia that all classes have come to accept it as part of the established order of things. A friend gave me a little dog to bring away with me. It was a valuable animal, and I wished to keep it with me. It is strictly forbidden to take dogs into railway carriages. The list of the pains and penalties for doing so frightened me considerably.

"Oh, that will be all right," my friend assured me; "have a few roubles loose in your pocket."

I tipped the station master and I tipped the guard, and started pleased with myself. But I had not anticipated what was in store for me. The news that an Englishman with a dog in a basket and roubles in his pocket was coming must have been telegraphed all down the line. At almost every stopping-place some enormous official, wearing generally a sword and a helmet, boarded the train. At first these fellows terrified me. I took them for field-marshals at least.

Visions of Siberia crossed my mind. Anxious and trembling, I gave the first one a gold piece. He shook me warmly by the hand—I thought he was going to kiss me. If I had offered him my cheek I am sure he would have done so. With the next one I felt less apprehensive. For a couple of roubles he blessed me, so I gathered; and, commending me to the care of the Almighty, departed. Before I had reached the German frontier, I was giving away the equivalent of English sixpences to men with the dress and carriage of major-generals; and to see their faces brighten up and to receive their heartfelt benediction was well worth the money.

But to the man without roubles in his pocket, Russian officialdom is not so gracious. By the expenditure of a few more coins I got my dog through the Customs without trouble, and had leisure to look about me. A miserable object was being badgered by half a dozen men in uniform, and he—his lean face puckered up into a snarl—was returning them snappish answers; the whole scene suggested some half-starved mongrel being worried by school-boys. A slight informality had been discovered in his passport, so a fellow traveller with whom I had made friends informed me. He had no roubles in his pocket, and in consequence they were sending him back to St. Petersburg—some eighteen hours' journey—in a wagon that in England would not be employed for the transport of oxen.

It seemed a good joke to Russian officialdom; they would drop in every now and then, look at him as he sat crouched in a corner of the waiting-room, and pass out again, laughing. The snarl had died from his face; a dull, listless indifference had taken its place—the look one sees on the face of a beaten dog, after the beating is over, when it is lying very still, its great eyes staring into nothingness, and one wonders whether it is thinking.

The Russian worker reads no newspaper, has no club, yet all things seem to be known to him. There is a prison on the banks of the Neva, in St. Petersburg. They say such things are done with now, but up till very recently there existed a small cell therein, below the level of the ice, and prisoners placed there would be found missing a day or two afterwards, nothing ever again known of them, except, perhaps, to the fishes of the Baltic. They talk of such like things among themselves: the sleigh-drivers round their charcoal fire, the field-workers going and coming in the grey dawn, the factory workers, their whispers deadened by the rattle of the looms.

I was searching for a house in Brussels some winters ago, and there was one I was sent to in a small street leading out of the Avenue Louise. It was poorly furnished, but rich in pictures, large and small. They covered the walls of every room.

"These pictures," explained to me the landlady, an old, haggard-looking woman, "will not be left, I am taking them with me to London. They are all the work of my husband. He is arranging an exhibition."

The friend who had sent me had told me the woman was a widow, who had been living in Brussels eking out a precarious existence as a lodging-house keeper for the last ten years.

"You have married again?" I questioned her.

The woman smiled.

"Not again. I was married eighteen years ago in Russia. My husband was transported to Siberia a few days after we were married, and I have never seen him since."

"I should have followed him," she added, "only every year we thought he was going to be set free."

"He is really free now?" I asked.

"Yes," she answered. "They set him free last week. He will join me in London. We shall be able to finish our honeymoon."

She smiled, revealing to me that once she had been a girl.

I read in the English papers of the exhibition in London. It was said the artist showed much promise. So possibly a career may at last be opening out for him.

Nature has made life hard to Russian rich and poor alike. To the banks of the Neva, with its ague and influenza-bestowing fogs and mists, one imagines that the Devil himself must have guided Peter the Great.

"Show me in all my dominions the most hopelessly unattractive site on which to build a city," Peter must have prayed; and the Devil having discovered the site on which St. Petersburg now stands, must have returned to his master in high good feather.

"I think, my dear Peter, I have found you something really unique. It is a pestilent swamp to which a mighty river brings bitter blasts and marrow-chilling fogs, while during the brief summer time the wind will bring you sand. In this way you will combine the disadvantages of the North Pole with those of the desert of Sahara."

In the winter time the Russians light their great stoves, and doubly barricade their doors and windows; and in this atmosphere, like to that of a greenhouse, many of their women will pass six months, never venturing out of doors. Even the men only go out at intervals. Every office, every shop is an oven. Men of forty have white hair and parchment faces; and the women are old at thirty. The farm labourers, during the few summer months, work almost entirely without sleep. They leave that for the winter, when they shut themselves up like dormice in their hovels, their store of food and vodka buried underneath the floor. For days together they sleep, then wake and dig, then sleep again.

The Russian party lasts all night. In an adjoining room are beds and couches; half a dozen guests are always sleeping. An hour contents them, then they rejoin the company, and other guests take their places. The Russian eats when he feels so disposed; the table is always spread, the guests come and go. Once a year there is a great feast in Moscow. The Russian merchant and his friends sit down early in the day, and a sort of thick, sweet pancake is served up hot. The feast continues for many hours, and the ambition of the Russian merchant is to eat more than his neighbour. Fifty or sixty of these hot cakes a man will consume at a sitting, and a dozen funerals in Moscow is often the result.

An uncivilised people, we call them in our lordly way, but they are young. Russian history is not yet three hundred years old. They will see us out, I am inclined to think. Their energy, their intelligence—when these show above the groundwork—are monstrous. I have known a Russian learn Chinese within six months. English! they learn it while you are talking to them. The children play at chess and study the violin for their own amusement.

The world will be glad of Russia—when she has put her house in order.

HOW TO BE HAPPY THOUGH LITTLE.

Folks suffering from Jingoism, Spreadeagleism, Chauvinism—all such like isms, to whatever country they belong—would be well advised to take a tour in Holland. It is the idea of the moment that size spells happiness. The bigger the country the better one is for living there. The happiest Frenchman cannot possibly be as happy as the most wretched Britisher, for the reason that Britain owns many more thousands of square miles than France possesses. The Swiss peasant, compared with the Russian serf, must, when he looks at the map of Europe and Asia, feel himself to be a miserable creature. The reason that everybody in America is happy and good is to be explained by the fact that America has an area equal to that of the entire moon. The American citizen who has backed the wrong horse, missed his train and lost his bag, remembers this and feels bucked up again.

According to this argument, fishes should be the happiest of mortals, the sea consisting—at least, so says my atlas: I have not measured it myself—of a hundred and forty-four millions of square miles. But, maybe, the sea is also divided in ways we wot not of. Possibly the sardine who lives near the Brittainy coast is sad and discontented because the Norwegian sardine is the proud inhabitant of a larger sea. Perhaps that is why he has left the Brittainy coast. Ashamed of being a Brittainy sardine, he has emigrated to Norway, has become a naturalized Norwegian sardine, and is himself again.

The happy Londoner on foggy days can warm himself with the reflection that the sun never sets on the British Empire. He does not often see the sun, but that is a mere detail. He regards himself as the owner of the sun; the sun begins his little day in the British Empire, ends his little day in the British Empire: for all practical purposes the sun is part of the British Empire. Foolish people in other countries sit underneath it and feel warm, but that is only their ignorance. They do not know it is a British possession; if they did they would feel cold.

My views on this subject are, I know, heretical. I cannot get it into my unpatriotic head that size is the only thing worth worrying about. In England, when I venture to express my out-of-date opinions, I am called a Little Englander. It fretted me at first; I was becoming a mere shadow. But by now I have got used to it. It would be the same, I feel, wherever I went. In New York I should be a Little American; in Constantinople a Little Turk. But I wanted to talk about Holland. A holiday in Holland serves as a corrective to exaggerated Imperialistic notions.

There are no poor in Holland. They may be an unhappy people, knowing what a little country it is they live in; but, if so, they hide the fact. To all seeming, the Dutch peasant, smoking his great pipe, is as much a man as the Whitechapel hawker or the moocher of the Paris boulevard. I saw a beggar once in Holland—in the townlet of Enkhuisen. Crowds were hurrying up from the side streets to have a look at him; the idea at first seemed to be that he was doing it for a bet. He turned out to be a Portuguese. They offered him work in the docks—until he could get something better to do—at wages equal in English money to about ten shillings a day. I inquired about him on my way back, and was told he had borrowed a couple of forms from the foreman and had left by the evening train. It is not the country for the loafer.

In Holland work is easily found; this takes away the charm of looking for it. A farm labourer in Holland lives in a brick-built house of six rooms, which generally belongs to him, with an acre or so of ground, and only eats meat once a day. The rest of his time he fills up on eggs and chicken and cheese and beer. But you rarely hear him grumble. His wife and daughter may be seen on Sundays wearing gold and silver jewellery worth from fifty to one hundred pounds, and there is generally enough old delft and pewter in the house to start a local museum anywhere outside Holland. On high days and holidays, of which in Holland there are plenty, the average Dutch vrouw would be well worth running away with. The Dutch peasant girl has no need of an illustrated journal once a week to tell her what the fashion is; she has it in the portrait of her mother, or of her grandmother, hanging over the glittering chimney-piece.

When the Dutchwoman builds a dress she builds it to last; it descends from mother to daughter, but it is made of sound material in the beginning. A lady friend of mine thought the Dutch costume would serve well for a fancy-dress ball, so set about buying one, but abandoned the notion on learning what it would cost her. A Dutch girl in her Sunday clothes must be worth fifty pounds before you come to ornaments. In certain provinces she wears a close-fitting helmet, made either of solid silver or of solid gold. The Dutch gallant, before making himself known, walks on tiptoe a little while behind the Loved One, and looks at himself in her head-dress just to make sure that his hat is on straight and his front curl just where it ought to be.

In most other European countries national costume is dying out. The slop-shop is year by year extending its hideous trade. But the country of Rubens and Rembrandt, of Teniers and Gerard Dow, remains still true to art. The picture post-card does not exaggerate. The men in those wondrous baggy knickerbockers, from the pockets of which you sometimes see a couple of chicken's heads protruding; in gaudy coloured shirts, in worsted hose and mighty sabots, smoking their great pipes—the women in their petticoats of many hues, in gorgeously embroidered vest, in chemisette of dazzling white, crowned with a halo of many frills, glittering in gold and silver—are not the creatures of an artist's fancy. You meet them in their thousands on holiday afternoons, walking gravely arm in arm, flirting with sober Dutch stolidity.

On colder days the women wear bright-coloured capes made of fine spun silk, from underneath the ample folds of which you sometimes hear a little cry; and sometimes a little hooded head peeps out, regards with preternatural thoughtfulness the toy-like world without, then dives back into shelter. As for the children—women in miniature, the single difference in dress being the gay pinafore—you can only say of them that they look like Dutch dolls. But such plump, contented, cheerful little dolls! You remember the hollow-eyed, pale-faced dolls you see swarming in the great, big and therefore should be happy countries, and wish that mere land surface were of less importance to our statesmen and our able editors, and the happiness and well-being of the mere human items worth a little more of their thought.

The Dutch peasant lives surrounded by canals, and reaches his cottage across a drawbridge. I suppose it is in the blood of the Dutch child not to tumble into a canal, and the Dutch mother never appears to anticipate such possibility. One can imagine the average English mother trying to bring up a family in a house surrounded by canals. She would never have a minute's peace until the children were in bed. But then the mere sight of a canal to the English child suggests the delights of a sudden and unexpected bath. I put it to a Dutchman once. Did the Dutch child by any chance ever fall into a canal?

"Yes," he replied, "cases have been known."

"Don't you do anything for it?" I enquired.

"Oh, yes," he answered, "we haul them out again."

"But what I mean is," I explained, "don't you do anything to prevent their falling in—to save them from falling in again?"

"Yes," he answered, "we spank 'em."

There is always a wind in Holland; it comes from over the sea. There is nothing to stay its progress. It leaps the low dykes and sweeps with a shriek across the sad, soft dunes, and thinks it is going to have a good time and play havoc in the land. But the Dutchman laughs behind his great pipe as it comes to him shouting and roaring. "Welcome, my hearty, welcome," he chuckles, "come blustering and bragging; the bigger you are the better I like you." And when it is once in the land, behind the long, straight dykes, behind the waving line of sandy dunes, he seizes hold of it, and will not let it go till it has done its tale of work.

The wind is the Dutchman's; servant before he lets it loose again it has turned ten thousand mills, has pumped the water and sawn the wood, has lighted the town and worked the loom, and forged the iron, and driven the great, slow, silent wherry, and played with the children in the garden. It is a sober wind when it gets back to sea, worn and weary, leaving the Dutchman laughing behind his everlasting pipe. There are canals in Holland down which you pass as though a field of wind-blown corn; a soft, low, rustling murmur ever in your ears. It is the ceaseless whirl of the great mill sails. Far out at sea the winds are as foolish savages, fighting, shrieking, tearing— purposeless. Here, in the street of mills, it is a civilized wind, crooning softly while it labours.

What charms one in Holland is the neatness and cleanliness of all about one. Maybe to the Dutchman there are drawbacks. In a Dutch household life must be one long spring-cleaning. No milk-pail is considered fit that cannot just as well be used for a looking-glass. The great brass pans, hanging under the pent house roof outside the cottage door, flash like burnished gold. You could eat your dinner off the red-tiled floor, but that the deal table, scrubbed to the colour of cream cheese, is more convenient. By each threshold stands a row of empty sabots, and woe-betide the Dutchman who would dream of crossing it in anything but his stockinged feet.

There is a fashion in sabots. Every spring they are freshly painted. One district fancies an orange yellow, another a red, a third white, suggesting purity and innocence. Members of the Smart Set indulge in ornamentation; a frieze in pink, a star upon the toe. Walking in sabots is not as easy as it looks. Attempting to run in sabots I do not recommend to the beginner.

"How do you run in sabots?" I asked a Dutchman once. I had been experimenting, and had hurt myself.

"We don't run," answered the Dutchman.

And observation has proved to me he was right. The Dutch boy, when he runs, puts them for preference on his hands, and hits other Dutch boys over the head with them as he passes.

The roads in Holland, straight and level, and shaded all the way with trees, look, from the railway-carriage window, as if they would be good for cycling; but this is a delusion. I crossed in the boat from Harwich once, with a well-known black and white artist, and an equally well-known and highly respected humorist. They had their bicycles with them, intending to tour Holland. I met them a fortnight later in Delft, or, rather, I met their remains. I was horrified at first. I thought it was drink. They could not stand still, they could not sit still, they trembled and shook in every limb, their teeth chattered when they tried to talk. The humorist hadn't a joke left in him. The artist could not have drawn his own salary; he would have dropped it on the way to his pocket. The Dutch roads are paved their entire length with cobbles—big, round cobbles, over which your bicycle leaps and springs and plunges.

If you would see Holland outside the big towns a smattering of Dutch is necessary. If you know German there is not much difficulty. Dutch—I speak as an amateur—appears to be very bad German mispronounced. Myself, I find my German goes well in Holland, even better than in Germany. The Anglo-Saxon should not attempt the Dutch G. It is hopeless to think of succeeding, and the attempt has been known to produce internal rupture. The Dutchman appears to keep his G in his stomach, and to haul it up when wanted. Myself, I find the ordinary G, preceded by a hiccough and followed by a sob, the nearest I can get to it. But they tell me it is not quite right, yet.

One needs to save up beforehand if one desires to spend any length of time in Holland. One talks of dear old England, but the dearest land in all the world is little Holland. The florin there is equal to the franc in France and to the shilling in England. They tell you that cigars are cheap in Holland. A cheap Dutch cigar will last you a day. It is not until you have forgotten the taste of it that you feel you ever want to smoke again. I knew a man who reckoned that he had saved hundreds of pounds by smoking Dutch cigars for a month steadily. It was years before he again ventured on tobacco.

Watching building operations in Holland brings home to you forc-ibly, what previously you have regarded as a meaningless formula—namely, that the country is built upon piles. A dozen feet below the level of the street one sees the labourers working in fishermen's boots up to their knees in water, driving the great wooden blocks into the mud. Many of the older houses slope forward at such an angle that you almost fear to pass beneath them. I should be as nervous as a kitten, living in one of the upper storeys. But the Dutchman leans out of a window that is hanging above the street six feet beyond the perpendicular, and smokes contentedly.

They have a merry custom in Holland of keeping the railway time twenty minutes ahead of the town time—or is it twenty minutes be-hind? I never can remember when I'm there, and I am not sure now. The Dutchman himself never knows.

"You've plenty of time," he says

"But the train goes at ten," you say; "the station is a mile away, and it is now half-past nine."

"Yes, but that means ten-twenty," he answers, "you have nearly an hour."

Five minutes later he taps you on the shoulder.

"My mistake, it's twenty to ten. I was thinking it was the other way about."

Another argues with him that his first idea was right. They work it out by scientific methods. Meanwhile you have dived into a cab. The result is always the same: you are either forty minutes too soon, or you have missed the train by twenty minutes. A Dutch platform is always crowded with women explaining volubly to their husbands either that there was not any need to have hurried, or else that the thing would have been to have started half an hour before they did, the man in both cases being, of course, to blame. The men walk up and down and swear.

The idea has been suggested that the railway time and the town time should be made to conform. The argument against the idea is that if it were carried out there would be nothing left to put the Dutchman out and worry him.

77

SHOULD WE SAY WHAT WE THINK,
OR THINK WHAT WE SAY?

A mad friend of mine will have it that the characteristic of the age is Make-Believe. He argues that all social intercourse is founded on make-believe. A servant enters to say that Mr. and Mrs. Bore are in the drawing-room.

"Oh, damn!" says the man.

"Hush!" says the woman. "Shut the door, Susan. How often am I to tell you never to leave the door open?"

The man creeps upstairs on tiptoe and shuts himself in his study. The woman does things before a looking-glass, waits till she feels she is sufficiently mistress of herself not to show her feelings, and then enters the drawing-room with outstretched hands and the look of one welcoming an angel's visit. She says how delighted she is to see the Bores—how good it was of them to come. Why did they not bring more Bores with them? Where is naughty Bore junior? Why does he never come to see her now? She will have to be really angry with him. And sweet little Flossie Bore? Too young to pay calls! Nonsense. An "At Home" day is not worth having where all the Bores are not.

The Bores, who had hoped that she was out—who have only called because the etiquette book told them that they must call at least four times in the season, explain how they have been trying and trying to come.

"This afternoon," recounts Mrs. Bore, "we were determined to come. 'John, dear,' I said this morning, 'I shall go and see dear Mrs. Bounder this afternoon, no matter what happens.'"

The idea conveyed is that the Prince of Wales, on calling at the Bores, was told that he could not come in. He might call again in the evening or come some other day.

That afternoon the Bores were going to enjoy themselves in their own way; they were going to see Mrs. Bounder.

"And how is Mr. Bounder?" demands Mrs. Bore.

Mrs. Bounder remains mute for a moment, straining her ears. She can hear him creeping past the door on his way downstairs. She hears the front door softly opened and closed-to. She wakes, as from a dream. She has been thinking of the sorrow that will fall on Bounder when he returns home later and learns what he has missed.

And thus it is, not only with the Bores and Bounders, but even with us who are not Bores or Bounders. Society in all ranks is founded on the make-believe that everybody is charming; that we are delighted to see everybody; that everybody is delighted to see us; that it is so good of everybody to come; that we are desolate at the thought that they really must go now.

Which would we rather do—stop and finish our cigar or hasten into the drawing-room to hear Miss Screecher sing? Can you ask us? We tumble over each other in our hurry. Miss Screecher would really rather not sing; but if we insist—We do insist. Miss Screecher, with pretty reluctance, consents. We are careful not to look at one another. We sit with our eyes fixed on the ceiling. Miss Screecher finishes, and rises.

"But it was so short," we say, so soon as we can be heard above the applause. Is Miss Screecher quite sure that was the whole of it? Or has she been playing tricks upon us, the naughty lady, defrauding us of a verse? Miss Screecher assures us that the fault is the composer's. But she knows another. At this hint, our faces lighten again with gladness. We clamour for more.

Our host's wine is always the most extraordinary we have ever tasted. No, not another glass; we dare not—doctor's orders, very strict. Our host's cigar! We did not know they made such cigars in this workaday world. No, we really could not smoke another. Well, if he will be so pressing, may we put it in our pocket? The truth is, we are not used to high smoking. Our hostess's coffee! Would she confide to us her secret? The baby! We hardly trust ourselves to speak. The usual baby—we have seen it. As a rule, to be candid, we never could detect much beauty in babies—have always held the usual gush about them to be insincere. But this baby! We are almost on the point of asking them where they got it. It is just the kind we wanted for ourselves. Little Janet's recitation: "A Visit to the Dentist!" Hitherto the amateur reciter has not appealed to us. But this is genius, surely. She ought to be trained for the stage.

Her mother does not altogether approve of the stage. We plead for the stage—that it may not be deprived of such talent.

Every bride is beautiful. Every bride looks charming in a simple costume of—for further particulars see local papers. Every marriage is a cause for universal rejoicing. With our wine-glass in our hand we picture the ideal life we know to be in store for them. How can it be otherwise? She, the daughter of her mother. (Cheers.) He— well, we all know him. (More cheers.) Also involuntary guffaw from ill-regulated young man at end of table, promptly suppressed.

We carry our make-believe even into our religion. We sit in church, and in voices swelling with pride, mention to the Almighty, at stated intervals, that we are miserable worms—that there is no good in us. This sort of thing, we gather, is expected of us; it does us no harm, and is supposed to please.

We make-believe that every woman is good, that every man is honest— until they insist on forcing us, against our will, to observe that they are not. Then we become very angry with them, and explain to them that they, being sinners, are not folk fit to mix with us perfect people. Our grief, when our rich aunt dies, is hardly to be borne. Drapers make fortunes, helping us to express feebly our desolation. Our only consolation is that she has gone to a better world.

Everybody goes to a better world when they have got all they can out of this one.

We stand around the open grave and tell each other so. The clergyman is so assured of it that, to save time, they have written out the formula for him and had it printed in a little book. As a child it used to surprise me—this fact that everybody went to heaven. Thinking of all the people that had died, I pictured the place overcrowded. Almost I felt sorry for the Devil, nobody ever coming his way, so to speak. I saw him in imagination, a lonely old gentleman, sitting at his gate day after day, hoping against hope, muttering to himself maybe that it hardly seemed worth while, from his point of view, keeping the show open. An old nurse whom I once took into my confidence was sure, if I continued talking in this sort of way, that he would get me anyhow. I must have been an evil-hearted youngster. The thought of how he would welcome me, the only human being that he had seen for years, had a certain fascination for me; for once in my existence I should be made a fuss about.

At every public meeting the chief speaker is always "a jolly good fellow." The man from Mars, reading our newspapers, would be convinced that every Member of Parliament was a jovial, kindly, high-hearted, generous-souled saint, with just sufficient humanity in him to prevent the angels from carrying him off bodily. Do not the entire audience, moved by one common impulse, declare him three times running, and in stentorian voice, to be this "jolly good fellow"? So say all of them. We have always listened with the most intense pleasure to the brilliant speech of our friend who has just sat down. When you thought we were yawning, we were drinking in his eloquence, open-mouthed.

The higher one ascends in the social scale, the wider becomes this necessary base of make-believe. When anything sad happens to a very big person, the lesser people round about him hardly care to go on living. Seeing that the world is somewhat overstocked with persons of impor- tance, and that something or another generally is happening to them, one wonders sometimes how it is the world continues to exist.

Once upon a time there occurred an illness to a certain good and great man. I read in my daily paper that the whole nation was plunged in grief. People dining in public restaurants, on being told the news by the waiter, dropped their heads upon the table and sobbed. Strangers, meeting in the street, flung their arms about one another and cried like little children. I was abroad at the time, but on the point of returning home. I almost felt ashamed to go. I looked at myself in the glass, and was shocked at my own appearance: it was that of a man who had not been in trouble for weeks. I felt that to burst upon this grief-stricken nation with a countenance such as mine would be to add to their sorrow. It was borne in upon me that I must have a shallow, egotistical nature. I had had luck with a play in America, and for the life of me I could not look grief-stricken. There were moments when, if I was not keeping a watch over myself, I found myself whistling.

Had it been possible I would have remained abroad till some stroke of ill-fortune had rendered me more in tune with my fellow-countrymen. But business was pressing. The first man I talked to on Dover pier was a Customs House official. You might have thought sorrow would have made him indifferent to a mere matter of forty-eight cigars. Instead of which, he appeared quite pleased when he found them. He demanded three-and-fourpence, and chuckled when he got it. On Dover platform a little girl laughed because a lady dropped a handbox on a dog; but then children are always callous—or, perhaps, she had not heard the news.

What astonished me most, however, was to find in the railway carriage a respectable looking man reading a comic journal. True, he did not laugh much: he had got decency enough for that; but what was a grief-stricken citizen doing with a comic journal, anyhow? Before

I had been in London an hour I had come to the conclusion that we English must be a people of wonderful self-control. The day before, according to the newspapers, the whole country was in serious danger of pining away and dying of a broken heart. In one day the nation had pulled itself together. "We have cried all day," they had said to themselves, "we have cried all night. It does not seem to have done much good. Now let us once again take up the burden of life." Some of them—I noticed it in the hotel dining-room that evening— were taking quite kindly to their food again.

We make believe about quite serious things. In war, each country's soldiers are always the most courageous in the world. The other country's soldiers are always treacherous and tricky; that is why they sometimes win. Literature is the art of make-believe.

"Now all of you sit round and throw your pennies in the cap," says the author, "and I will pretend that there lives in Bayswater a young lady named Angelina, who is the most beautiful young lady that ever existed. And in Notting Hill, we will pretend, there resides a young man named Edwin, who is in love with Angelina."

And then, there being sufficient pennies in the cap, the author starts away, and pretends that Angelina thought this and said that, and that Edwin did all sorts of wonderful things. We know he is making it all up as he goes along. We know he is making up just what he thinks will please us. He, on the other hand, has to make-believe that he is doing it because he cannot help it, he being an artist. But we know well enough that, were we to stop throwing the pennies into the cap, he would find out precious soon that he could.

The theatrical manager bangs his drum.

"Walk up! walk up!" he cries, "we are going to pretend that Mrs. Johnson is a princess, and old man Johnson is going to pretend to be a pirate. Walk up, walk up, and be in time!"

So Mrs. Johnson, pretending to be a princess, comes out of a wobbly thing that we agree to pretend is a castle; and old man Johnson, pretending to be a pirate, is pushed up and down on another wobbly thing that we agree to pretend is the ocean. Mrs. Johnson pretends to be in love with him, which we know she is not. And Johnson pretends to be a very terrible person; and Mrs. Johnson pretends, till eleven o'clock, to believe it. And we pay prices, varying from a shilling to half-a-sovereign, to sit for two hours and listen to them.

But as I explained at the beginning, my friend is a mad sort of person.

IS THE AMERICAN HUSBAND MADE
ENTIRELY OF STAINED GLASS.

I am glad I am not an American husband. At first sight this may appear a remark uncomplimentary to the American wife. It is nothing of the sort. It is the other way about. We, in Europe, have plenty of opportunity of judging the American wife. In America you hear of the American wife, you are told stories about the American wife, you see her portrait in the illustrated journals. By searching under the heading "Foreign Intelligence," you can find out what she is doing. But here in Europe we know her, meet her face to face, talk to her, flirt with her. She is charming, delightful. That is why I say I am glad I am not an American husband. If the American husband only knew how nice was the American wife, he would sell his business and come over here, where now and then he could see her.

Years ago, when I first began to travel about Europe, I argued to myself that America must be a deadly place to live in. How sad it is, I thought to myself, to meet thus, wherever one goes, American widows by the thousand. In one narrow by-street of Dresden I calculated fourteen American mothers, possessing nine-and-twenty American children, and not a father among them—not a single husband among the whole fourteen. I pictured fourteen lonely graves, scattered over the United States. I saw as in a vision those fourteen head-stones of best material, hand-carved, recording the virtues of those fourteen dead and buried husbands.

Odd, thought I to myself, decidedly odd. These American husbands, they must be a delicate type of humanity. The wonder is their mothers ever reared them. They marry fine girls, the majority of them; two or three sweet children are born to them, and after that there appears to be no further use for them, as far as this world is concerned. Can nothing be done to strengthen their constitutions? Would a tonic be of any help to them? Not the customary tonic, I don't mean, the sort of tonic merely intended to make gouty old gentlemen feel they want to buy a hoop, but the sort of tonic for which it was claimed that three drops poured upon a ham sandwich and the thing would begin to squeak.

It struck me as pathetic, the picture of these American widows leaving their native land, coming over in shiploads to spend the rest of their blighted lives in exile. The mere thought of America, I took it, had for ever become to them distasteful. The ground that once his feet had pressed! The old familiar places once lighted by his smile! Everything in America would remind them of him. Snatching their babes to their heaving bosoms they would leave the country where lay buried all the joy of their lives, seek in the retirement of Paris, Florence or Vienna, oblivion of the past.

Also, it struck me as beautiful, the noble resignation with which they bore their grief, hiding their sorrow from the indifferent stranger. Some widows make a fuss, go about for weeks looking gloomy and depressed, making not the slightest effort to be merry. These fourteen widows—I knew them personally, all of them, I lived in the same street—what a brave show of cheerfulness they put on! What a lesson to the common or European widow, the humpy type of widow! One could spend whole days in their company—I had done it—commencing quite early in the morning with a sleighing excursion, finishing up quite late in the evening with a little supper party, followed by an impromptu dance; and never detect from their outward manner that they were not thoroughly enjoying themselves.

From the mothers I turned my admiring eyes towards the children. This is the secret of American success, said I to myself; this high-spirited courage, this Spartan contempt for suffering. Look at them! the gallant little men and women. Who would think that they had lost a father? Why, I have seen a British child more upset at losing sixpence.

Talking to a little girl one day, I enquired of her concerning the health of her father. The next moment I could have bitten my tongue out, remembering that there wasn't such a thing as a father—not an American father—in the whole street. She did not burst into tears as they do in the story-books. She said:

"He is quite well, thank you," simply, pathetically, just like that.

"I am sure of it," I replied with fervour, "well and happy as he deserves to be, and one day you will find him again; you will go to him."

"Ah, yes," she answered, a shining light, it seemed to me, upon her fair young face. "Momma says she is getting just a bit tired of this one-horse sort of place. She is quite looking forward to seeing him again."

It touched me very deeply: this weary woman, tired of her long bereavement, actually looking forward to the fearsome passage leading to where her loved one waited for her in a better land.

For one bright breezy creature I grew to feel a real regard. All the months that I had known her, seen her almost daily, never once had I heard a single cry of pain escape her lips, never once had I heard her cursing fate. Of the many who called upon her in her charming flat, not one had ever, to my knowledge, offered her consolation or condolence. It seemed to me cruel, callous. The over-burdened heart, finding no outlet for its imprisoned grief, finding no sympathetic ear into which to pour its tale of woe, breaks, we are told; anyhow, it isn't good for it. I decided—no one else seeming keen—that I would supply that sympathetic ear. The very next time I found myself alone with her I introduced the subject.

"You have been living here in Dresden a long time, have you not?" I asked.

"About five years," she answered, "on and off."

"And all alone," I commented, with a sigh intended to invite to confidence.

"Well, hardly alone," she corrected me, while a look of patient resignation added dignity to her piquant features. "You see, there are the dear children always round about me, during the holidays."

"Besides," she added, "the people here are real kind to me; they hardly ever let me feel myself alone. We make up little parties, you know, picnics and excursions. And then, of course, there is the Opera and the Symphony Concerts, and the subscription dances. The dear old king has been doing a good deal this winter, too; and I must say the Embassy folks have been most thoughtful, so far as I am concerned. No, it would not be right for me to complain of loneliness, not now that I have got to know a few people, as it were."

"But don't you miss your husband?" I suggested.

A cloud passed over her usually sunny face. "Oh, please don't talk of him," she said, "it makes me feel real sad, thinking about him."

But having commenced, I was determined that my sympathy should not be left to waste.

"What did he die of?" I asked.

She gave me a look the pathos of which I shall never forget.

"Say, young man," she cried, "are you trying to break it to me gently? Because if so, I'd rather you told me straight out. What did he die of?"

"Then isn't he dead?" I asked, "I mean so far as you know."

"Never heard a word about his being dead till you started the idea," she retorted. "So far as I know he's alive and well."

I said that I was sorry. I went on to explain that I did not mean I was sorry to hear that in all probability he was alive and well. What I meant was I was sorry I had introduced a painful subject.

"What's a painful subject?"

"Why, your husband," I replied.

"But why should you call him a painful subject?"

I had an idea she was getting angry with me. She did not say so. I gathered it. But I had to explain myself somehow.

"Well," I answered, "I take it, you didn't get on well together, and I am sure it must have been his fault."

"Now look here," she said, "don't you breathe a word against my husband or we shall quarrel. A nicer, dearer fellow never lived."

"Then what did you divorce him for?" I asked. It was impertinent, it was unjustifiable. My excuse is that the mystery surrounding the American husband had been worrying me for months. Here had I stumbled upon the opportunity of solving it. Instinctively I clung to my advantage.

"There hasn't been any divorce," she said. "There isn't going to be any divorce. You'll make me cross in another minute."

But I was becoming reckless. "He is not dead. You are not divorced from him. Where is he?" I demanded with some heat.

"Where is he?" she replied, astonished. Where should he be? At home, of course." I looked around the luxuriously-furnished room with its air of cosy comfort, of substantial restfulness.

"What home?" I asked.

"What home! Why, our home, in Detroit."

"What is he doing there?" I had become so much in earnest that my voice had assumed unconsciously an authoritative tone. Presumably, it hypnotised her, for she answered my questions as though she had been in the witness-box.

"How do I know? How can I possibly tell you what he is doing? What do people usually do at home?"

"Answer the questions, madam, don't ask them. What are you doing here? Quite truthfully, if you please." My eyes were fixed upon her.

"Enjoying myself. He likes me to enjoy myself. Besides, I am educating the children."

"You mean they are here at boarding-school while you are gadding about. What is wrong with American education? When did you see your husband last?"

"Last? Let me see. No, last Christmas I was in Berlin. It must have been the Christmas before, I think."

"If he is the dear kind fellow you say he is, how is it you haven't seen him for two years?"

"Because, as I tell you, he is at home, in Detroit. How can I see him when I am here in Dresden and he is in Detroit? You do ask foolish questions. He means to try and come over in the summer, if he can spare the time, and then, of course—

"Answer my questions, please. I've spoken to you once about it. Do you think you are performing your duty as a wife, enjoying yourself in Dresden and Berlin while your husband is working hard in Detroit?"

"He was quite willing for me to come. The American husband is a good fellow who likes his wife to enjoy herself."

"I am not asking for your views on the American husband. I am asking your views on the American wife—on yourself. The American husband appears to be a sort of stained-glass saint, and you American wives are imposing upon him. It is doing you no good, and it won't go on for ever. There will come a day when the American husband will wake up to the fact he is making a fool of himself, and by over-indulgence, over-devotion, turning the American woman into a heartless, selfish creature. What sort of a home do you think it is in Detroit, with you and the children over here? Tell me, is the American husband made entirely of driven snow, with blood distilled from moonbeams, or is he composed of the ordinary ingredients? Because, if the latter, you take my advice and get back home. I take it that in America, proper, there are millions of real homes where the woman does her duty and plays the game. But also it is quite clear there are thousands of homes in America, mere echoing rooms, where the man walks by himself, his wife and children scattered over Europe. It isn't going to work, it isn't right that it should work."

"You take the advice of a sincere friend. Pack up—you and the children—and get home."

I left. It was growing late. I felt it was time to leave. Whether she took my counsel I cannot say. I only know that there still remain in Europe a goodly number of American wives to whom it is applicable.

DOES THE YOUNG MAN KNOW
EVERYTHING WORTH KNOWING?

I am told that American professors are "mourning the lack of ideals" at Columbia University—possibly also at other universities scattered through the United States. If it be any consolation to these mourning American professors, I can assure them that they do not mourn alone. I live not far from Oxford, and enjoy the advantage of occasionally listening to the jeremiads of English University professors. More than once a German professor has done me the honour to employ me as an object on which to sharpen his English. He also has mourned similar lack of ideals at Heidelberg, at Bonn. Youth is youth all the world over; it has its own ideals; they are not those of the University professor. The explanation is tolerably simple. Youth is young, and the University professor, generally speaking, is middle-aged.

I can sympathise with the mourning professor. I, in my time, have suffered like despair. I remember the day so well; it was my twelfth birthday. I recall the unholy joy with which I reflected that for the future my unfortunate parents would be called upon to pay for me full railway fare; it marked a decided step towards manhood. I was now in my teens. That very afternoon there came to visit us a relative of ours. She brought with her three small children: a girl, aged six; a precious, golden-haired thing in a lace collar that called itself a boy, aged five; and a third still smaller creature, it might have been male, it might have been female; I could not have told you at the time, I cannot tell you now. This collection of atoms was handed over to me.

"Now, show yourself a man," said my dear mother, "remember you are in your teens. Take them out for a walk and amuse them; and mind nothing happens to them."

To the children themselves their own mother gave instructions that they were to do everything that I told them, and not to tear their clothes or make themselves untidy. These directions, even to myself, at the time, appeared contradictory. But I said nothing. And out into the wilds the four of us departed.

I was an only child. My own infancy had passed from my memory. To me, at twelve, the ideas of six were as incomprehensible as are those of twenty to the University professor of forty. I wanted to be a pirate. Round the corner and across the road building operations were in progress. Planks and poles lay ready to one's hand. Nature, in the neighbourhood, had placed conveniently a shallow pond. It was Saturday afternoon. The nearest public-house was a mile away. Immunity from interference by the British workman was thus assured. It occurred to me that by placing my three depressed looking relatives on one raft, attacking them myself from another, taking the eldest girl's sixpence away from her, disabling their raft, and leaving them to drift without a rudder, innocent amusement would be provided for half an hour at least.

They did not want to play at pirates. At first sight of the pond the thing that called itself a boy began to cry. The six-year-old lady said she did not like the smell of it. Not even after I had explained the game to them were they any the more enthusiastic for it.

I proposed Red Indians. They could go to sleep in the unfinished building upon a sack of lime, I would creep up through the grass, set fire to the house, and dance round it, whooping and waving my tomahawk, watching with fiendish delight the frantic but futile efforts of the pale-faces to escape their doom.

It did not "catch on"—not even that. The precious thing in the lace collar began to cry again. The creature concerning whom I could not have told you whether it was male or female made no attempt at argument, but started to run; it seemed to have taken a dislike to this particular field. It stumbled over a scaffolding pole, and then it also began to cry. What could one do to amuse such people? I left it to them to propose something. They thought they would like to play at "Mothers"—not in this field, but in some other field.

The eldest girl would be mother. The other two would represent her children. They had been taken suddenly ill. "Waterworks," as I had christened him, was to hold his hands to his middle and groan. His face brightened up at the suggestion. The nondescript had the toothache. It took up its part without a moment's hesitation, and set to work to scream. I could be the doctor and look at their tongues.

That was their "ideal" game. As I have said, remembering that afternoon, I can sympathise with the University professor mourning the absence of University ideals in youth. Possibly at six my own ideal game may have been "Mothers." Looking back from the pile of birthdays upon which I now stand, it occurs to me that very probably it was. But from the perspective of twelve, the reflection that there were beings in the world who could find recreation in such fooling saddened me.

Eight years later, his father not being able to afford the time, I conducted Master "Waterworks," now a healthy, uninteresting, gawky lad, to a school in Switzerland. It was my first Continental trip. I should have enjoyed it better had he not been with me. He thought Paris a "beastly hole." He did not share my admiration for the Frenchwoman; he even thought her badly dressed.

"Why she's so tied up, she can't walk straight," was the only impression she left upon him.

We changed the subject; it irritated me to hear him talk. The beautiful Juno-like creatures we came across further on in Germany, he said were too fat. He wanted to see them run. I found him utterly soulless.

To expect a boy to love learning and culture is like expecting him to prefer old vintage claret to gooseberry wine. Culture for the majority is an acquired taste. Speaking personally, I am entirely in agreement with the University professor. I find knowledge, prompting to observation and leading to reflection, the most satisfactory luggage with which a traveller through life can provide himself. I would that I had more of it. To be able to enjoy a picture is of more advantage than to be able to buy it.

All that the University professor can urge in favour of idealism I am prepared to endorse. But then I am—let us say, thirty-nine. At fourteen my candid opinion was that he was talking "rot." I looked at the old gentleman himself—a narrow-chested, spectacled old gentleman, who lived up a by street. He did not seem to have much fun of any sort. It was not my ideal. He told me things had been written in a language called Greek that I should enjoy reading, but I had not even read all Captain Marryat. There were tales by Sir Walter Scott and "Jack Harkaway's Schooldays!" I felt I could wait a while. There was a chap called Aristophanes who had written comedies, satirising the political institutions of a country that had disappeared two thousand years ago. I say, without shame, Drury Lane pantomime and Barnum's Circus called to me more strongly.

Wishing to give the old gentleman a chance, I dipped into translations. Some of these old fellows were not as bad as I had imagined them.

A party named Homer had written some really interesting stuff. Here and there, maybe, he was a bit long-winded, but, taking him as a whole, there was "go" in him. There was another of them—Ovid was his name. He could tell a story, Ovid could. He had imagination. He was almost as good as "Robinson Crusoe." I thought it would please my professor, telling him that I was reading these, his favourite authors.

"Reading them!" he cried, "but you don't know Greek or Latin."

"But I know English," I answered; "they have all been translated into English. You never told me that!"

It appeared it was not the same thing. There were subtle delicacies of diction bound to escape even the best translator. These subtle delicacies of diction I could enjoy only by devoting the next seven or eight years of my life to the study of Greek and Latin. It will grieve the University professor to hear it, but the enjoyment of those subtle delicacies of diction did not appear to me—I was only fourteen at the time, please remember—to be worth the time and trouble.

The boy is materially inclined—the mourning American professor has discovered it. I did not want to be an idealist living up a back street. I wanted to live in the biggest house in the best street of the town. I wanted to ride a horse, wear a fur coat, and have as much to eat and drink as ever I liked. I wanted to marry the most beautiful woman in the world, to have my name in the newspaper, and to know that everybody was envying me.

Mourn over it, my dear professor, as you will—that is the ideal of youth; and, so long as human nature remains what it is, will continue to be so. It is a materialistic ideal—a sordid ideal. Maybe it is necessary. Maybe the world would not move much if the young men started thinking too early. They want to be rich, so they fling themselves frenziedly into the struggle. They build the towns, and make the railway tracks, hew down the forests, dig the ore out of the ground. There comes a day when it is borne in upon them that trying to get rich is a poor sort of game—that there is only one thing more tiresome than being a millionaire, and that is trying to be a millionaire. But, meanwhile, the world has got its work done.

The American professor fears that the artistic development of America leaves much to be desired. I fear the artistic development of most countries leaves much to be desired. Why the Athenians themselves sandwiched their drama between wrestling competitions and boxing bouts. The plays of Sophocles, or Euripides, were given as "side shows." The chief items of the fair were the games and races. Besides,

America is still a young man. It has been busy "getting on in the world." It has not yet quite finished. Yet there are signs that young America is approaching the thirty-nines. He is finding a little time, a little money to spare for art. One can almost hear young America—not quite so young as he was—saying to Mrs. Europe as he enters and closes the shop door:

"Well, ma'am, here I am, and maybe you'll be glad to hear I've a little money to spend. Yes, ma'am, I've fixed things all right across the water; we shan't starve. So now, ma'am, you and I can have a chat concerning this art I've been hearing so much about. Let's have a look at it, ma'am, trot it out, and don't you be afraid of putting a fair price upon it."

I am inclined to think that Mrs. Europe has not hesitated to put a good price upon the art she has sold to Uncle Sam. I am afraid Mrs. Europe has occasionally "unloaded" on Uncle Sam. I talked to a certain dealer one afternoon, now many years ago, at the Uwantit Club.

"What is the next picture likely to be missing?" I asked him in the course of general conversation.

"Thome little thing of Hoppner'th, if it mutht be," he replied with confidence.

"Hoppner," I murmured, "I seem to have heard the name."

"Yeth; you'll hear it a bit oftener during the next eighteen month or tho. You take care you don't get tired of hearing it, thath all," he laughed. "Yeth," he continued, thoughtfully, "Reynoldth ith played out. Nothing much to be made of Gainthborough, either. Dealing in that lot now, why, it'th like keeping a potht offith. Hoppner'th the coming man."

"You've been buying Hoppners up cheap," I suggested.

"Between uth," he answered, "yeth, I think we've got them all. Maybe a few more. I don't think we've mithed any."

"You will sell them for more than you gave for them," I hinted.

"You're thmart," he answered, regarding me admiringly, "you thee through everything you do."

"How do you work it?" I asked him. There is a time in the day when he is confidential. "Here is this man, Hoppner. I take it that you have bought him up at an average of a hundred pounds a picture, and that at that price most owners were fairly glad to sell. Few folks outside the art schools have ever heard of him. I bet that at the present moment there isn't one art critic who could spell his name without reference to a dictionary. In eighteen months you will be selling him for anything from one thousand to ten thousand pounds. How is it done?"

"How ith everything done that'th done well?" he answered. "By ear-netht effort." He hitched his chair nearer to me, "I get a chap— one of your thort of chapth—he writ'th an article about Hoppner. I get another to anthwer him. Before I've done there'll be a hundred articleth about Hoppner—hith life, hith early thruggie, anecdo'th about hith wife. Then a Hoppner will be thold at public auchtion for a thouthand guineath."

"But how can you be certain it will fetch a thousand guineas?" I interrupted.

"I happen to know the man whoth going to buy it." He winked, and I understood.

"A fortnight later there will be a thale of half-a-dothen, and the prithe will be gone up by that time."

"And after that?" I said.

"After that," he replied, rising, "the American millionaire! He'll jutht be waiting on the door-thtep for the thale-room to open."

"If by any chance I come across a Hoppner?" I said, laughing, as I turned to go.

"Don't you hold on to it too long, that'th all," was his advice.

HOW MANY CHARMS HATH MUSIC, WOULD YOU SAY?

The argument of the late Herr Wagner was that grand opera—the music drama, as he called it—included, and therefore did away with the necessity for—all other arts. Music in all its branches, of course, it provides: so much I will concede to the late Herr Wagner. There are times, I confess, when my musical yearnings might shock the late Herr Wagner—times when I feel unequal to following three distinct themes at one and the same instant.

"Listen," whispers the Wagnerian enthusiast to me, "the cornet has now the Brunnhilda motive." It seems to me, in my then state of depravity, as if the cornet had even more than this the matter with him.

"The second violins," continues the Wagnerian enthusiast, "are carrying on the Wotan theme." That they are carrying on goes without saying: the players' faces are streaming with perspiration.

"The brass," explains my friend—his object is to cultivate my ear—"is accompanying the singers." I should have said drowning them. There are occasions when I can rave about Wagner with the best of them. High class moods come to all of us. The difference between the really high-class man and us commonplace, workaday men is the difference between, say, the eagle and the barnyard chicken. I am the barnyard chicken. I have my wings. There are ecstatic moments when I feel I want to spurn the sordid earth and soar into the realms of art. I do fly a little, but my body is heavy, and I only get as far as the fence. After a while I find it lonesome on the fence, and I hop down again among my fellows.

Listening to Wagner, during such temporary Philistinic mood, my sense of fair play is outraged. A lone, lorn woman stands upon the stage trying to make herself heard. She has to do this sort of thing for her living; maybe an invalid mother, younger brothers and sisters are dependent upon her. One hundred and forty men, all armed with powerful instruments, well-organised, and most of them looking well-fed, combine to make it impossible for a single note of that poor woman's voice to be heard above their din. I see her standing there, opening and shutting her mouth, getting redder and redder in the face. She is singing, one feels sure of it; one could hear her if only those one hundred and forty men would ease up for a minute. She makes one mighty, supreme effort; above the banging of the drums, the blare of the trumpets, the shrieking of the strings, that last despairing note is distinctly heard.

She has won, but the victory has cost her dear. She sinks down fainting on the stage and is carried off by supers. Chivalrous indignation has made it difficult for me to keep my seat watching the unequal contest. My instinct was to leap the barrier, hurl the bald-headed chief of her enemies from his high chair, and lay about me with the trombone or the clarionet—whichever might have come the easier to my snatch.

"You cowardly lot of bullies," I have wanted to cry, "are you not ashamed of yourselves? A hundred and forty of you against one, and that one a still beautiful and, comparatively speaking, young lady. Be quiet for a minute—can't you? Give the poor girl a chance."

A lady of my acquaintance says that sitting out a Wagnerian opera seems to her like listening to a singer accompanied by four orchestras playing different tunes at the same time. As I have said, there are times when Wagner carries me along with him, when I exult in the crash and whirl of his contending harmonies. But, alas! there are those other moods—those after dinner moods—when my desire is for something distinctly resembling a tune. Still, there are other composers of grand opera besides Wagner. I grant to the late Herr Wagner, that, in so far as music is concerned, opera can supply us with all we can need.

But it was also Wagner's argument that grand opera could supply us with acting, and there I am compelled to disagree with him. Wagner thought that the arts of acting and singing could be combined. I have seen artists the great man has trained himself. As singers they left nothing to be desired, but the acting in grand opera has never yet impressed me. Wagner never succeeded in avoiding the operatic convention and nobody else ever will. When the operatic lover meets his sweetheart he puts her in a corner and, turning his back upon her, comes down to the footlights and tells the audience how he adores her. When he has finished, he, in his turn, retires into the corner, and she comes down and tells the audience that she is simply mad about him.

Overcome with joy at finding she really cares for him, he comes down right and says that this is the happiest moment of his life; and she stands left, twelve feet away from him, and has the presentiment that all this sort of thing is much too good to last. They go off together, backwards, side by side. If there is any love-making, such as I understand by the term, it is done "off." This is not my idea of acting. But I do not see how you are going to substitute for it anything more natural. When you are singing at the top of your voice, you don't want a heavy woman hanging round your neck. When you are killing a man and warbling about it at the same time, you don't want him fooling around you defending himself. You want him to have a little reasonable patience, and to wait in his proper place till you have finished, telling him, or rather telling the crowd, how much you hate and despise him.

When the proper time comes, and if he is where you expect to find him while thinking of your upper C, you will hit him lightly on the shoulder with your sword, and then he can die to his own particular tune. If you have been severely wounded in battle, or in any other sort of row, and have got to sing a long ballad before you finally expire, you don't want to have to think how a man would really behave who knew he had only got a few minutes to live and was feeling bad about it. The chances are that he would not want to sing at all. The woman who really loved him would not encourage him to sing. She would want him to keep quiet while she moved herself about a bit, in case there was anything that could be done for him.

If a mob is climbing the stairs thirsting for your blood, you do not want to stand upright with your arms stretched out, a good eighteen inches from the door, while you go over at some length the varied incidents leading up to the annoyance. If your desire were to act naturally you would push against that door for all you were worth, and yell for somebody to bring you a chest of drawers and a bedstead, and things like that, to pile up against it. If you were a king, and were giving a party, you would not want your guests to fix you up at the other end of the room and leave you there, with nobody to talk to but your own wife, while they turned their backs upon you, and had a long and complicated dance all to themselves. You would want to be in it; you would want to let them know that you were king.

In acting, all these little points have to be considered. In opera, everything is rightly sacrificed to musical necessity. I have seen the young, enthusiastic opera-singer who thought that he or she could act and sing at the same time. The experienced artist takes the centre of the stage and husbands his resources. Whether he is supposed to be indignant because somebody has killed his mother, or cheerful because he is going out to fight his country's foes, who are only waiting until he has finished singing to attack the town, he leaves it to the composer to make clear.

Also it was Herr Wagner's idea that the back cloth would leave the opera-goer indifferent to the picture gallery. The castle on the rock, accessible only by balloon, in which every window lights up simultaneously and instantaneously, one minute after sunset, while the full moon is rushing up the sky at the pace of a champion comet— that wonderful sea that suddenly opens and swallows up the ship— those snow-clad mountains, over which the shadow of the hero passes like a threatening cloud—the grand old chateau, trembling in the wind—what need, will ask the opera-goer of the future, of your Turners and your Corots, when, for prices ranging from a shilling upwards, we can have a dozen pictures such as these rolled up and down before us every evening?

But perhaps the most daring hope of all was the dream that came to Herr Wagner that his opera singers, his grouped choruses, would eventually satisfy the craving of the public for high class statuary. I am not quite sure the general public does care for statuary. I do not know whether the idea has ever occurred to the Anarchist, but, were I myself organising secret committee meetings for unholy purposes, I should invite my comrades to meet in that section of the local museum devoted to statuary. I can conceive of no place where we should be freer from prying eyes and listening ears. A select few, however, do appreciate statuary; and such, I am inclined to think, will not be weaned from their passion by the contemplation of the opera singer in his or her various quaint costumes.

And even if the tenor always satisfied our ideal of Apollo, and the soprano were always as sylph-like as she is described in the libretto, even then I should doubt the average operatic chorus being regarded by the connoisseur as a cheap and pleasant substitute for a bas relief from the Elgin marbles. The great thing required of that operatic chorus is experience. The young and giddy-pated the chorus master has no use for. The sober, honest, industrious lady or gentleman, with a knowledge of music is very properly his ideal.

What I admire about the chorus chiefly is its unity. The whole village dresses exactly alike. In wicked, worldly villages there is rivalry, leading to heartburn and jealously. One lady comes out suddenly, on, say, a Bank Holiday, in a fetching blue that conquers every male heart. Next holiday her rival cuts her out with a green hat. In the operatic village it must be that the girls gather together beforehand to arrange this thing. There is probably a meeting called.

"The dear Count's wedding," announces the chairwoman, "you will all be pleased to hear, has been fixed for the fourteenth, at eleven o'clock in the morning. The entire village will be assembled at ten-thirty to await the return of the bridal cortege from the church, and offer its felicitations. Married ladies, will, of course, come accompanied by their husbands. Unmarried ladies must each bring a male partner as near their own height as possible. Fortunately, in this village the number of males is exactly equal to that of females, so that the picture need not be spoiled. The children will organise themselves into an independent body and will group themselves picturesquely. It has been thought advisable," continues the chairwoman, "that the village should meet the dear Count and his bride at some spot not too far removed from the local alehouse. The costume to be worn by the ladies will consist of a short pink skirt terminating at the knees and ornamented with festoons of flowers; above will be worn a bolero in mauve silk without sleeves and cut decollete. The shoes should be of yellow satin over flesh-coloured stockings. Ladies who are 'out' will wear pearl necklaces, and a simple device in emeralds to decorate the hair. Thank God, we can all of us afford it, and provided the weather holds up and nothing unexpected happens—he is not what I call a lucky man, our Count, and it is always as well to be prepared for possibilities—well, I think we may look forward to a really pleasant day."

It cannot be done, Herr Wagner, believe me. You cannot substitute the music drama for all the arts combined. The object to be aimed at by the wise composer should be to make us, while listening to his music, forgetful of all remaining artistic considerations.

THE WHITE MAN'S BURDEN! NEED IT BE SO HEAVY?

It is a delightful stroll on a sunny summer morning from the Hague to the Huis ten Bosch, the little "house in the wood," built for Princess Amalia, widow of Stadtholter Frederick Henry, under whom Holland escaped finally from the bondage of her foes and entered into the promised land of Liberty. Leaving the quiet streets, the tree-bordered canals, with their creeping barges, you pass through a pleasant park, where the soft-eyed deer press round you, hurt and indignant if you have brought nothing in your pocket—not even a piece of sugar—to offer them. It is not that they are grasping—it is the want of attention that wounds them.

"I thought he was a gentleman," they seem to be saying to one another, if you glance back, "he looked like a gentleman."

Their mild eyes haunt you; on the next occasion you do not forget. The Park merges into the forest; you go by winding ways till you reach the trim Dutch garden, moat-encircled, in the centre of which stands the prim old-fashioned villa, which, to the simple Dutchman, appears a palace. The concierge, an old soldier, bows low to you and introduces you to his wife—a stately, white-haired dame, who talks most languages a little, so far as relates to all things within and appertaining to this tiny palace of the wood. To things without, beyond the wood, her powers of conversation do not extend: apparently such matters do not interest her.

She conducts you to the Chinese Room; the sun streams through the windows, illuminating the wondrous golden dragons standing out in bold relief from the burnished lacquer work, decorating still further with light and shade the delicate silk embroideries thin taper hands have woven with infinite pains. The walls are hung with rice paper, depicting the conventional scenes of the conventional Chinese life.

You find your thoughts wandering. These grotesque figures, these caricatures of humanity! A comical creature, surely, this Chinaman, the pantaloon of civilization. How useful he has been to us for our farces, our comic operas! This yellow baby, in his ample pinafore, who lived thousands of years ago, who has now passed into this strange second childhood.

But is he dying—or does the life of a nation wake again, as after sleep? Is he this droll, harmless thing he here depicts himself? And if not? Suppose fresh sap be stirring through his three hundred millions? We thought he was so very dead; we thought the time had come to cut him up and divide him, the only danger being lest we should quarrel over his carcase among ourselves.

Suppose it turns out as the fable of the woodcutter and the bear? The woodcutter found the bear lying in the forest. At first he was much frightened, but the bear lay remarkably still. So the woodman crept nearer, ventured to kick the bear—very gently, ready to run if need be. Surely the bear was dead! And parts of a bear are good to eat, and bearskin to poor woodfolk on cold winter nights is grateful. So the woodman drew his knife and commenced the necessary preliminaries. But the bear was not dead.

If the Chinaman be not dead? If the cutting-up process has only served to waken him? In a little time from now we shall know.

From the Chinese Room the white-haired dame leads us to the Japanese Room. Had gentle-looking Princess Amalia some vague foreshadowing of the future in her mind when she planned these two rooms leading into one another? The Japanese decorations are more grotesque, the designs less cheerfully comical than those of cousin Chinaman. These monstrous, mis-shapen wrestlers, these patient-looking gods, with their inscrutable eyes! Was it always there, or is it only by the light of present events that one reads into the fantastic fancies of the artist working long ago in the doorway of his paper house, a meaning that has hitherto escaped us?

But the chief attraction of the Huis ten Bosch is the gorgeous Orange Saloon, lighted by a cupola, fifty feet above the floor, the walls one blaze of pictures, chiefly of the gorgeous Jordaen school—"The Defeat of the Vices," "Time Vanquishing Slander"—mostly allegorical, in praise of all the virtues, in praise of enlightenment and progress. Aptly enough in a room so decorated, here was held the famous Peace Congress that closed the last century. One can hardly avoid smiling as one thinks of the solemn conclave of grandees assembled to proclaim the popularity of Peace.

It was in the autumn of the same year that Europe decided upon the dividing-up of China, that soldiers were instructed by Christian monarchs to massacre men, women and children, the idea being to impress upon the Heathen Chinee the superior civilization of the white man. The Boer war followed almost immediately. Since when the white man has been pretty busy all over the world with his "expeditions" and his "missions." The world is undoubtedly growing more refined. We do not care for ugly words. Even the burglar refers airily to the "little job" he has on hand. You would think he had found work in the country. I should not be surprised to learn that he says a prayer before starting, telegraphs home to his anxious wife the next morning that his task has been crowned with blessing.

Until the far-off date of Universal Brotherhood war will continue. Matters considered unimportant by both parties will—with a mighty flourish of trumpets—be referred to arbitration. I was talking of a famous financier a while ago with a man who had been his secretary. Amongst other anecdotes, he told me of a certain agreement about which dispute had arisen. The famous financier took the paper into his own hands and made a few swift calculations.

"Let it go," he concluded, "it is only a thousand pounds at the outside. May as well be honest."

Concerning a dead fisherman or two, concerning boundaries through unproductive mountain ranges we shall arbitrate and feel virtuous. For gold mines and good pasture lands, mixed up with a little honour to give respectability to the business, we shall fight it out, as previously. War being thus inevitable, the humane man will rejoice that by one of those brilliant discoveries, so simple when they are explained, war in the future is going to be rendered equally satisfactory to victor and to vanquished.

In by-elections, as a witty writer has pointed out, there are no defeats—only victories and moral victories. The idea seems to have caught on. War in the future is evidently going to be conducted on the same understanding. Once upon a time, from a far-off land, a certain general telegraphed home congratulating his Government that the enemy had shown no inclination whatever to prevent his running away. The whole country rejoiced.

"Why, they never even tried to stop him," citizens, meeting other citizens in the street, told each other. "Ah, they've had enough of him. I bet they are only too glad to get rid of him. Why, they say he ran for miles without seeing a trace of the foe."

The enemy's general, on the other hand, also wrote home congratulating his Government. In this way the same battle can be mafficked over by both parties. Contentment is the great secret of happiness. Everything happens for the best, if only you look at it the right way. That is going to be the argument. The general of the future will telegraph to headquarters that he is pleased to be able to inform His Majesty that the enemy, having broken down all opposition, has succeeded in crossing the frontier and is now well on his way to His Majesty's capital.

"I am luring him on," he will add, "as fast as I can. At our present rate of progress, I am in hopes of bringing him home by the tenth."

Lest foolish civilian sort of people should wonder whereabouts lies the cause for rejoicing, the military man will condescend to explain. The enemy is being enticed farther and farther from his base. The defeated general—who is not really defeated, who is only artful, and who appears to be running away, is not really running away at all. On the contrary, he is running home—bringing, as he explains, the enemy with him.

If I remember rightly—it is long since I played it—there is a parlour game entitled "Puss in the Corner." You beckon another player to you with your finger. "Puss, puss!" you cry. Thereupon he has to leave his chair—his "base," as the military man would term it—and try to get to you without anything happening to him.

War in the future is going to be Puss in the Corner on a bigger scale. You lure your enemy away from his base. If all goes well—if he does not see the trap that is being laid for him—why, then, almost before he knows it, he finds himself in your capital. That finishes the game. You find out what it is he really wants. Provided it is something within reason, and you happen to have it handy, you give it to him. He goes home crowing, and you, on your side, laugh when you think how cleverly you succeeded in luring him away from his base.

There is a bright side to all things. The gentleman charged with the defence of a fortress will meet the other gentleman who has captured it and shake hands with him mid the ruins.

"So here you are at last!" he will explain. "Why didn't you come before? We have been waiting for you."

And he will send off dispatches felicitating his chief on having got that fortress off their hands, together with all the worry and expense it has been to them. When prisoners are taken you will console yourself with the reflection that the cost of feeding them for the future will have to be borne by the enemy. Captured cannon you will watch being trailed away with a sigh of relief.

"Confounded heavy things!" you will say to yourself. "Thank goodness I've got rid of them. Let him have the fun of dragging them about these ghastly roads. See how he likes the job!"

War is a ridiculous method of settling disputes. Anything that can tend to make its ridiculous aspect more apparent is to be welcomed. The new school of military dispatch-writers may succeed in turning even the laughter of the mob against it.

The present trouble in the East would never have occurred but for the white man's enthusiasm for bearing other people's burdens. What we call the yellow danger is the fear that the yellow man may before long request us, so far as he is concerned, to put his particular burden down. It may occur to him that, seeing it is his property, he would just as soon carry it himself. A London policeman told me a story the other day that struck him as an example of Cockney humour under trying circumstances. But it may also serve as a fable. From a lonely street in the neighbourhood of Covent Garden, early one morning, the constable heard cries of "Stop thief!" shouted in a childish treble. He arrived on the scene just in time to collar a young hooligan, who, having snatched a basket of fruit from a small lad—a greengrocer's errand boy, as it turned out—was, with it, making tracks. The greengrocer's boy, between panting and tears, delivered his accusation. The hooligan regarded him with an expression of amazed indignation.

"What d'yer mean, stealing it?" exclaimed Mr. Hooligan. "Why, I was carrying it for yer!"

The white man has got into the way of "carrying" other people's burdens, and now it looks as if the yellow man were going to object to our carrying his any further. Maybe he is going to get nasty, and insist on carrying it himself. We call this "the yellow danger."

A friend of mine—he is a man who in the street walks into lamp-posts, and apologises—sees rising from the East the dawn of a new day in the world's history. The yellow danger is to him a golden hope. He sees a race long stagnant, stretching its giant limbs with the first vague movements of returning life. He is a poor sort of patriot; he calls himself, I suppose, a white man, yet he shamelessly confesses he would rather see Asia's millions rise from the ruins of their ancient civilization to take their part in the future of humanity, than that half the population of the globe should remain bound in savagery for the pleasure and the profit of his own particular species.

He even goes so far as to think that the white man may have something to learn. The world has belonged to him now for some thousands of years. Has he done all with it that could have been done? Are his ideals the last word?

Not what the yellow man has absorbed from Europe, but what he is going to give Europe it is that interests my friend. He is watching the birth of a new force—an influence as yet unknown. He clings to the fond belief that new ideas, new formulae, to replace the old worn shibboleths, may, during these thousands of years, have been developing in those keen brains that behind the impressive yellow mask have been working so long in silence and in mystery.

WHY DIDN'T HE MARRY THE GIRL?

What is wrong with marriage, anyhow? I find myself pondering this question so often, when reading high-class literature. I put it to myself again the other evening, during a performance of Faust. Why could not Faust have married the girl? I would not have married her myself for any consideration whatsoever; but that is not the argument. Faust, apparently, could not see anything amiss with her. Both of them were mad about each other. Yet the idea of a quiet, unostentatious marriage with a week's honeymoon, say, in Vienna, followed by a neat little cottage orne, not too far from Nurnberg, so that their friends could have come out to them, never seems to have occurred to either of them.

There could have been a garden. Marguerite might have kept chickens and a cow. That sort of girl, brought up to hard work and by no means too well educated, is all the better for having something to do. Later, with the gradual arrival of the family, a good, all-round woman might have been hired in to assist. Faust, of course, would have had his study and got to work again; that would have kept him out of further mischief. The idea that a brainy man, his age, was going to be happy with nothing to do all day but fool round a petticoat was ridiculous from the beginning. Valentine—a good fellow, Valentine, with nice ideas—would have spent his Saturdays to Monday with them. Over a pipe and a glass of wine, he and Faust would have discussed the local politics.

He would have danced the children on his knee, have told them tales about the war—taught the eldest boy to shoot. Faust, with a practical man like Valentine to help him, would probably have invented a new gun. Valentine would have got it taken up.

Things might have come of it. Sybil, in course of time, would have married and settled down—perhaps have taken a little house near to them. He and Marguerite would have joked—when Mrs. Sybil was not around—about his early infatuation. The old mother would have tod-dled over from Nurnberg—not too often, just for the day.

The picture grows upon one the more one thinks of it. Why did it never occur to them? There would have been a bit of a bother with the Old Man. I can imagine Mephistopheles being upset about it, thinking him-self swindled. Of course, if that was the reason—if Faust said to himself:

"I should like to marry the girl, but I won't do it; it would not be fair to the Old Man; he has been to a lot of trouble working this thing up; in common gratitude I cannot turn round now and behave like a decent, sensible man; it would not be playing the game"—if this was the way Faust looked at the matter there is nothing more to be said. Indeed, it shows him in rather a fine light—noble, if quixotic.

If, on the other hand, he looked at the question from the point of view of himself and the girl, I think the thing might have been man-aged. All one had to do in those days when one wanted to get rid of the Devil was to show him a sword hilt. Faust and Marguerite could have slipped into a church one morning, and have kept him out of the way with a sword hilt till the ceremony was through. They might have hired a small boy:

"You see the gentleman in red? Well, he wants us and we don't want him. That is the only difference between us. Now, you take this sword, and when you see him coming show him the hilt. Don't hurt him; just show him the sword and shake your head. He will understand."

The old gentleman's expression, when subsequently Faust presented him to Marguerite, would have been interesting:

"Allow me, my wife. My dear, a—a friend of mine. You may remem-ber meeting him that night at your aunt's."

As I have said, there would have been ructions; but I do not myself see what could have been done. There was nothing in the bond to the effect that Faust should not marry, so far as we are told. The Old Man had a sense of humour. My own opinion is that, after getting over the first annoyance, he himself would have seen the joke. I can even picture him looking in now and again on Mr. and Mrs. Faust. The children would be hurried off to bed. There would be, for a while, an atmosphere of constraint.

But the Old Man had a way with him. He would have told one or two stories at which Marguerite would have blushed, at which Faust would have grinned. I can see the old fellow occasionally joining the homely social board. The children, awed at first, would have sat silent, with staring eyes. But, as I have said, the Old Man had a way with him.

Why should he not have reformed? The good woman's unconsciously exerted influence—the sweet childish prattle! One hears of such things. Might he not have come to be known as "Nunkie"?

Myself—I believe I have already mentioned it—I would not have married Marguerite. She is not my ideal of a good girl. I never liked the way she deceived her mother. And that aunt of hers! Well, a nice girl would not have been friends with such a woman. She did not behave at all too well to Sybil, either. It is clear to me that she led the boy on. And what was she doing with that box of jewels, anyhow? She was not a fool. She could not have gone every day to that fountain, chatted with those girl friends of hers, and learnt nothing. She must have known that people don't go leaving twenty thousand pounds' worth of jewels about on doorsteps as part of a round game. Her own instinct, if she had been a good girl, would have told her to leave the thing alone.

I don't believe in these innocent people who do not know what they are doing half their time. Ask any London magistrate what he thinks of the lady who explains that she picked up the diamond brooch:-

"Not meaning, of course, your Worship, to take it. I would not do such a thing. It just happened this way, your Worship. I was standing as you might say here, and not seeing anyone about in the shop I opened the case and took it out, thinking as perhaps it might belong to someone; and then this gentleman here, as I had not noticed before, comes up quite suddenly and says; 'You come along with me,' he says. 'What for,' I says, 'when I don't even know you?' I says. 'For stealing,' he says. 'Well, that's a hard word to use to a lady,' I says; 'I don't know what you mean, I'm sure.'"

And if she had put them all on, not thinking, what would a really nice girl have done when the gentleman came up and assured her they were hers? She would have been thirty seconds taking them off and flinging them back into the box.

"Thank you," she would have said, "I'll trouble you to leave this garden as quickly as you entered it and take them with you. I'm not that sort of girl."

Marguerite clings to the jewels, and accepts the young man's arm for a moonlight promenade. And when it does enter into her innocent head that he and she have walked that shady garden long enough, what does she do when she has said good-bye and shut the door? She opens the ground-floor window and begins to sing!

Maybe I am not poetical, but I do like justice. When other girls do these sort of things they get called names. I cannot see why this particular girl should be held up as an ideal. She kills her mother. According to her own account this was an accident. It is not an original line of defence, and we are not allowed to hear the evidence for the prosecution. She also kills her baby. You are not to blame her for that, because at the time she was feeling poorly. I don't see why this girl should have a special line of angels to take her up to heaven. There must have been decent, hard-working women in Nurnburg more entitled to the ticket.

Why is it that all these years we have been content to accept Marguerite as a type of innocence and virtue? The explanation is, I suppose, that Goethe wrote at a time when it was the convention to regard all women as good. Anything in petticoats was virtuous. If she did wrong it was always somebody else's fault. Cherchez la femme was a later notion. In the days of Goethe it was always Cherchez l'homme. It was the man's fault. It was the devil's fault. It was anybody's fault you liked, but not her's.

The convention has not yet died out. I was reading the other day a most interesting book by a brilliant American authoress. Seeing I live far away from the lady's haunts, I venture to mention names. I am speaking of "Patience Sparhawk," by Gertrude Atherton. I take this book because it is typical of a large body of fiction. Miss Sparhawk lives a troubled life: it puzzles her. She asks herself what is wrong. Her own idea is that it is civilisation.

If it is not civilisation, then it is the American man or Nature—or Democracy. Miss Sparhawk marries the wrong man. Later on she gets engaged to another wrong man. In the end we are left to believe she is about to be married to the right man. I should be better satisfied if I could hear Miss Sparhawk talking six months after that last marriage. But if a mistake has again been made I am confident that, in Miss Sparhawk's opinion, the fault will not be Miss Sparhawk's. The argument is always the same: Miss Sparhawk, being a lady, can do no wrong.

If Miss Sparhawk cared to listen to me for five minutes, I feel I could put her right on this point.

"It is quite true, my dear girl," I should say to her, "something is wrong—very wrong. But it is not the American man. Never you mind the American man: you leave him to worry out his own salvation. You are not the girl to put him right, even where he is wrong. And it is not civilisation. Civilisation has a deal to answer for, I admit: don't you load it up with this additional trouble. The thing that is wrong in this case of yours—if you will forgive my saying so—is you. You make a fool of yourself; you marry a man who is a mere animal because he appeals to your animal instincts. Then, like the lady who cried out 'Alack, I've married a black,' you appeal to heaven against the injustice of being mated with a clown. You are not a nice girl, either in your ideas or in your behaviour. I don't blame you for it; you did not make yourself. But when you set to work to attract all that is lowest in man, why be so astonished at your own success? There are plenty of shocking American men, I agree. One meets the class even outside America. But nice American girls will tell you that there are also nice American men. There is an old proverb about birds of a feather. Next time you find yourself in the company of a shocking American man, you just ask yourself how he got there, and how it is he seems to be feeling at home. You learn self-control. Get it out of your head that you are the centre of the universe, and grasp the idea that a petticoat is not a halo, and you will find civilisation not half as wrong as you thought it."

I know what Miss Sparhawk's reply would be.

"You say all this to me—to me, a lady? Great Heavens! What has become of chivalry?"

A Frenchman was once put on trial for murdering his father and mother. He confessed his guilt, but begged for mercy on the plea that he was an orphan. Chivalry was founded on the assumption that woman was worthy to be worshipped. The modern woman's notion is that when she does wrong she ought to be excused by chivalrous man because she is a lady.

I like the naughty heroine; we all of us do. The early Victorian heroine—the angel in a white frock, was a bore. We knew exactly what she was going to do—the right thing. We did not even have to ask ourselves, "What will she think is the right thing to do under the circumstances?" It was always the conventional right thing. You could have put it to a Sunday school and have got the answer every time. The heroine with passions, instincts, emotions, is to be welcomed. But I want her to grasp the fact that after all she is only one of us. I should like her better if, instead of demanding:

"What is wrong in civilisation? What is the world coming to?" and so forth, she would occasionally say to herself:

"Guess I've made a fool of myself this time. I do feel that 'shamed of myself."

She would not lose by it. We should respect her all the more.

WHAT MRS. WILKINS THOUGHT ABOUT IT.

Last year, travelling on the Underground Railway, I met a man; he was one of the saddest-looking men I had seen for years. I used to know him well in the old days when we were journalists together. I asked him, in a sympathetic tone, how things were going with him. I expected his response would be a flood of tears, and that in the end I should have to fork out a fiver. To my astonishment, his answer was that things were going exceedingly well with him. I did not want to say to him bluntly:

"Then what has happened to you to make you look like a mute at a temperance funeral?" I said:

"And how are all at home?"

I thought that if the trouble lay there he would take the opportunity. It brightened him somewhat, the necessity of replying to the question. It appeared that his wife was in the best of health.

"You remember her," he continued with a smile; "wonderful spirits, always cheerful, nothing seems to put her out, not even—"

He ended the sentence abruptly with a sigh.

His mother-in-law, I learned from further talk with him, had died since I had last met him, and had left them a comfortable addition to their income. His eldest daughter was engaged to be married.

"It is entirely a love match," he explained, "and he is such a dear, good fellow, that I should not have made any objection even had he been poor. But, of course, as it is, I am naturally all the more content."

His eldest boy, having won the Mottle Scholarship, was going up to Cambridge in the Autumn. His own health, he told me, had greatly improved; and a novel he had written in his leisure time promised to be one of the successes of the season. Then it was that I spoke plainly.

"If I am opening a wound too painful to be touched," I said, "tell me. If, on the contrary, it is an ordinary sort of trouble upon which the sympathy of a fellow worker may fall as balm, let me hear it."

"So far as I am concerned," he replied, "I should be glad to tell you. Speaking about it does me good, and may lead—so I am always in hopes—to an idea. But, for your own sake, if you take my advice, you will not press me."

"How can it affect me?" I asked, "it is nothing to do with me, is it?"

"It need have nothing to do with you," he answered, "if you are sensible enough to keep out of it. If I tell you: from this time onward it will be your trouble also. Anyhow, that is what has happened in four other separate cases. If you like to be the fifth and complete the half dozen of us, you are welcome. But remember I have warned you."

"What has it done to the other five?" I demanded.

"It has changed them from cheerful, companionable persons into gloomy one-idead bores," he told me. "They think of but one thing, they talk of but one thing, they dream of but one thing. Instead of getting over it, as time goes on, it takes possession of them more and more. There are men, of course, who would be unaffected by it— who could shake it off. I warn you in particular against it, because, in spite of all that is said, I am convinced you have a sense of humour; and that being so, it will lay hold of you. It will plague you night and day. You see what it has made of me! Three months ago a lady interviewer described me as of a sunny temperament. If you know your own business you will get out at the next station."

I wish now I had followed his advice. As it was, I allowed my curiosity to take possession of me, and begged him to explain. And he did so.

"It was just about Christmas time," he said. "We were discussing the Drury Lane Pantomime—some three or four of us—in the smoking room of the Devonshire Club, and young Gold said he thought it would prove a mistake, the introduction of a subject like the Fiscal question into the story of Humpty Dumpty. The two things, so far as he could see, had nothing to do with one another. He added that he entertained a real regard for Mr. Dan Leno, whom he had once met on a steamboat, but that there were other topics upon which he would prefer to seek that gentleman's guidance. Nettleship, on the other hand, declared that he had no sympathy with the argument that artists should never intrude upon public affairs. The actor was a fellow citizen with the rest of us. He said that, whether one agreed with their conclusions or not, one must admit that the nation owed a debt of gratitude to Mrs. Brown Potter and to Miss Olga Nethersole for giving to it the benefit of their convictions. He had talked to both ladies in private on the subject and was convinced they knew as much about it as did most people.

"Burnside, who was one of the party, contended that if sides were to be taken, a pantomime should surely advocate the Free-Food Cause, seeing it was a form of entertainment supposed to appeal primarily to the tastes of the Little Englander. Then I came into the discussion.

"'The Fiscal question,' I said, 'is on everybody's tongue. Such being the case, it is fit and proper it should be referred to in our annual pantomime, which has come to be regarded as a review of the year's doings. But it should not have been dealt with from the political standpoint. The proper attitude to have assumed towards it was that of innocent raillery, free from all trace of partisanship.'

"Old Johnson had strolled up and was standing behind us.

"'The very thing I have been trying to get hold of for weeks,' he said—'a bright, amusing resume of the whole problem that should give offence to neither side. You know our paper,' he continued; 'we steer clear of politics, but, at the same time, try to be up-to-date; it is not always easy. The treatment of the subject, on the lines you suggest, is just what we require. I do wish you would write me something.'

"He is a good old sort, Johnson; it seemed an easy thing. I said I would. Since that time I have been thinking how to do it. As a matter of fact, I have not thought of much else. Maybe you can suggest something."

I was feeling in a good working mood the next morning.

"Pilson," said I to myself, "shall have the benefit of this. He does not need anything boisterously funny. A few playfully witty remarks on the subject will be the ideal."

I lit a pipe and sat down to think. At half-past twelve, having to write some letters before going out to lunch, I dismissed the Fiscal question from my mind.

But not for long. It worried me all the afternoon. I thought, maybe, something would come to me in the evening. I wasted all that evening, and I wasted all the following morning. Everything has its amusing side, I told myself. One turns out comic stories about funerals, about weddings. Hardly a misfortune that can happen to mankind but has produced its comic literature. An American friend of mine once took a contract from the Editor of an Insurance Journal to write four humorous stories; one was to deal with an earthquake, the second with a cyclone, the third with a flood, and the fourth with a thunderstorm. And more amusing stories I have never read. What is the matter with the Fiscal question?

I myself have written lightly on Bime-metallism. Home Rule we used to be merry over in the eighties. I remember one delightful evening at the Codgers' Hall. It would have been more delightful still, but for a raw-boned Irishman, who rose towards eleven o'clock and requested to be informed if any other speaker was wishful to make any more jokes on the subject of Ould Ireland; because, if so, the raw-boned gentleman was prepared to save time by waiting and dealing with them altogether. But if not, then—so the raw-boned gentleman announced—his intention was to go for the last speaker and the last speaker but two at once and without further warning.

No other humourist rising, the raw-boned gentleman proceeded to make good his threat, with the result that the fun degenerated somewhat. Even on the Boer War we used to whisper jokes to one another in quiet places. In this Fiscal question there must be fun. Where is it?

For days I thought of little else. My laundress—as we call them in the Temple—noticed my trouble.

"Mrs. Wilkins," I confessed, "I am trying to think of something innocently amusing to say on the Fiscal question."

"I've 'eard about it," she said, "but I don't 'ave much time to read the papers. They want to make us pay more for our food, don't they?"

"For some of it," I explained. "But, then, we shall pay less for other things, so that really we shan't be paying more at all."

"There don't seem much in it, either way," was Mrs. Wilkins' opinion.

"Just so," I agreed, "that is the advantage of the system. It will cost nobody anything, and will result in everybody being better off."

"The pity is," said Mrs. Wilkins "that pity nobody ever thought of it before."

"The whole trouble hitherto," I explained, "has been the foreigner."

"Ah," said Mrs. Wilkins, "I never 'eard much good of 'em, though they do say the Almighty as a use for almost everything."

"These foreigners," I continued, "these Germans and Americans, they dump things on us, you know."

"What's that?" demanded Mrs. Wilkins.

"What's dump? Well, it's dumping, you know. You take things, and you dump them down."

"But what things? 'Ow do they do it?" asked Mrs. Wilkins.

"Why, all sorts of things: pig iron, bacon, door-mats—everything. They bring them over here—in ships, you understand—and then, if you please, just dump them down upon our shores."

"You don't mean surely to tell me that they just throw them out and leave them there?" queried Mrs. Wilkins.

"Of course not," I replied; "when I say they dump these things upon our shores, that is a figure of speech. What I mean is they sell them to us."

"But why do we buy them if we don't want them?" asked Mrs. Wilkins; "we're not bound to buy them, are we?"

"It is their artfulness," I explained, "these Germans and Americans, and the others; they are all just as bad as one another—they insist on selling us these things at less price than they cost to make."

"It seems a bit silly of them, don't it?" thought Mrs. Wilkins. "I suppose being foreigners, poor things, they ain't naturally got much sense."

"It does seem silly of them, if you look at it that way," I admitted, "but what we have got to consider is, the injury it is doing us."

"Don't see 'ow it can do us much 'arm," argued Mrs. Wilkins; "seems a bit of luck so far as we are concerned. There's a few more things they'd be welcome to dump round my way."

"I don't seem to be putting this thing quite in the right light to you, Mrs. Wilkins," I confessed. "It is a long argument, and you might not be able to follow it; but you must take it as a fact now generally admitted that the cheaper you buy things the sooner your money goes. By allowing the foreigner to sell us all these things at about half the cost price, he is getting richer every day, and we are getting poorer. Unless we, as a country, insist on paying at least twenty per cent. more for everything we want, it is calculated that in a very few years England won't have a penny left."

"Sounds a bit topsy turvy," suggested Mrs. Wilkins.

"It may sound so," I answered, "but I fear there can be no doubt of it. The Board of Trade Returns would seem to prove it conclusively."

"Well, God be praised, we've found it out in time," ejaculated Mrs. Wilkins piously.

"It is a matter of congratulation," I agreed; "the difficulty is that a good many other people say that far from being ruined, we are doing very well indeed, and are growing richer every year."

"But 'ow can they say that," argued Mrs. Wilkins, "when, as you tell me, those Trade Returns prove just the opposite?"

"Well, they say the same, Mrs. Wilkins, that the Board of Trade Returns prove just the opposite."

"Well, they can't both be right," said Mrs. Wilkins.

"You would be surprised, Mrs. Wilkins," I said, "how many things can be proved from Board of Trade Returns!"

But I have not yet thought of that article for Pilson.

SHALL WE BE RUINED BY CHINESE CHEAP LABOUR?

"*What* is all this talk I 'ear about the Chinese?" said Mrs. Wilkins to me the other morning. We generally indulge in a little chat while Mrs. Wilkins is laying the breakfast-table. Letters and newspapers do not arrive in my part of the Temple much before nine. From half-past eight to nine I am rather glad of Mrs. Wilkins. "They 'ave been up to some of their tricks again, 'aven't they?"

"The foreigner, Mrs. Wilkins," I replied, "whether he be Chinee or any other he, is always up to tricks. Was not England specially prepared by an all-wise Providence to frustrate these knavish tricks? Which of such particular tricks may you be referring to at the moment, Mrs. Wilkins?"

"Well, 'e's comin' over 'ere—isn't he, sir? to take the work out of our mouths, as it were."

"Well, not exactly over here, to England, Mrs. Wilkins," I explained. "He has been introduced into Africa to work in the mines there."

"It's a funny thing," said Mrs. Wilkins, "but to 'ear the way some of them talk in our block, you might run away with the notion—that is, if you didn't know 'em—that work was their only joy. I said to one of 'em, the other evening—a man as calls 'isself a brass finisher, though, Lord knows, the only brass 'e ever finishes is what 'is poor wife earns and isn't quick enough to 'ide away from 'im—well, whatever 'appens, I says, it will be clever of 'em if they take away much work from you. It made them all laugh, that did," added Mrs. Wilkins, with a touch of pardonable pride.

"Ah," continued the good lady, "it's surprising 'ow contented they can be with a little, some of 'em. Give 'em a 'ard-working woman to look after them, and a day out once a week with a procession of the un-employed, they don't ask for nothing more. There's that beauty my poor sister Jane was fool enough to marry. Serves 'er right, as I used to tell 'er at first, till there didn't seem any more need to rub it into 'er. She'd 'ad one good 'usband. It wouldn't 'ave been fair for 'er to 'ave 'ad another, even if there'd been a chance of it, seeing the few of 'em there is to go round among so many. But it's always the same with us widows: if we 'appen to 'ave been lucky the first time, we put it down to our own judg-ment—think we can't ever make a mistake; and if we draw a wrong 'un, as the saying is, we argue as if it was the duty of Providence to make it up to us the second time. Why, I'd a been making a fool of myself three years ago if 'e 'adn't been good-natured enough to call one afternoon when I was out, and 'ook it off with two pounds eight in the best teapot that I 'ad been soft enough to talk to 'im about: and never let me set eyes on 'im again. God bless 'im! 'E's one of the born-tireds, 'e is, as poor Jane might 'ave seen for 'erself, if she 'ad only looked at 'im, instead of listening to 'im.

"But that's courtship all the world over—old and young alike, so far as I've been able to see it," was the opinion of Mrs. Wilkins. "The man's all eyes and the woman all ears. They don't seem to 'ave any other senses left 'em. I ran against 'im the other night, on my way 'ome, at the corner of Gray's Inn Road. There was the usual crowd watching a pack of them Italians laying down the asphalt in 'Olborn, and 'e was among 'em. 'E 'ad secured the only lamp-post, and was leaning agen it.

"'Ullo,' I says, 'glad to see you 'aven't lost your job. Nothin' like stick-in' to it, when you've dropped into somethin' that really suits you.'

"'What do you mean, Martha?' 'e says. 'E's not one of what I call your smart sort. It takes a bit of sarcasm to get through 'is 'ead.

"'Well,' I says, 'you're still on the old track, I see, looking for work. Take care you don't 'ave an accident one of these days and run up agen it before you've got time to get out of its way.'

"'It's these miserable foreigners,' 'e says. 'Look at 'em,' 'e says.

"'There's enough of you doing that,' I says. 'I've got my room to put straight and three hours needlework to do before I can get to bed. But don't let me 'inder you. You might forget what work was like, if you didn't take an opportunity of watching it now and then.'

"'They come over 'ere,' 'e says, 'and take the work away from us chaps.'

"'Ah,' I says, 'poor things, perhaps they ain't married.'

"'Lazy devils! 'e says. 'Look at 'em, smoking cigarettes. I could do that sort of work. There's nothing in it. It don't take 'eathen foreigners to dab a bit of tar about a road.'

"'Yes,' I says, 'you always could do anybody else's work but your own.'

"'I can't find it, Martha,' 'e says.

"'No,' I says, 'and you never will in the sort of places you go looking for it. They don't 'ang it out on lamp-posts, and they don't leave it about at the street corners. Go 'ome,' I says, 'and turn the mangle for your poor wife. That's big enough for you to find, even in the dark.'

"Looking for work!" snorted Mrs. Wilkins with contempt; "we women never 'ave much difficulty in finding it, I've noticed. There are times when I feel I could do with losing it for a day."

"But what did he reply, Mrs. Wilkins," I asked; "your brass-finishing friend, who was holding forth on the subject of Chinese cheap labour." Mrs. Wilkins as a conversationalist is not easily kept to the point. I was curious to know what the working classes were thinking on the subject.

"Oh, that," replied Mrs. Wilkins, "'e did not say nothing. 'E ain't the sort that's got much to say in an argument. 'E belongs to the crowd that 'angs about at the back, and does the shouting. But there was another of 'em, a young fellow as I feels sorry for, with a wife and three small children, who 'asn't 'ad much luck for the last six months; and that through no fault of 'is own, I should say, from the look of 'im. 'I was a fool,' says 'e, 'when I chucked a good situation and went out to the war. They told me I was going to fight for equal rights for all white men. I thought they meant that all of us were going to 'ave a better chance, and it seemed worth making a bit of sacrifice for, that did. I should be glad if they would give me a job in their mines that would enable me to feed my wife and children. That's all I ask them for!'"

"It is a difficult problem, Mrs. Wilkins," I said. "According to the mine owners—"

"Ah," said Mrs. Wilkins. "They don't seem to be exactly what you'd call popular, them mine owners, do they? Daresay they're not as bad as they're painted."

"Some people, Mrs. Wilkins," I said, "paint them very black. There are those who hold that the South African mine-owner is not a man at all, but a kind of pantomime demon. You take Goliath, the whale that swallowed Jonah, a selection from the least respectable citizens of Sodom and Gomorrah at their worst, Bluebeard, Bloody Queen Mary, Guy Fawkes, and the sea-serpent—or, rather, you take the most objectionable attributes of all these various personages, and mix them up together. The result is the South African mine-owner, a monster who would willingly promote a company for the putting on the market of a new meat extract, prepared exclusively from new-born infants, provided the scheme promised a fair and reasonable opportunity of fleecing the widow and orphan."

"I've 'eard they're a bad lot," said Mrs. Wilkins. "But we're most of us that, if we listen to what other people say about us."

"Quite so, Mrs. Wilkins," I agreed. "One never arrives at the truth by listening to one side only. On the other hand, for example, there are those who stoutly maintain that the South African mine-owner is a kind of spiritual creature, all heart and sentiment, who, against his own will, has been, so to speak, dumped down upon this earth as the result of over-production up above of the higher class of archangel. The stock of archangels of superior finish exceeds the heavenly demand; the surplus has been dropped down into South Africa and has taken to mine owning. It is not that these celestial visitors of German sounding nomenclature care themselves about the gold. Their only desire is, during this earthly pilgrimage of theirs, to benefit the human race. Nothing can be obtained in this world without money—"

"That's true," said Mrs. Wilkins, with a sigh.

"For gold, everything can be obtained. The aim of the mine-owning archangel is to provide the world with gold. Why should the world trouble to grow things and make things? 'Let us,' say these archangels, temporarily dwelling in South Africa, 'dig up and distribute to the world plenty of gold, then the world can buy whatever it wants, and be happy.'

"There may be a flaw in the argument, Mrs. Wilkins," I allowed. "I am not presenting it to you as the last word upon the subject. I am merely quoting the view of the South African mine-owner, feeling himself a much misunderstood benefactor of mankind."

"I expect," said Mrs. Wilkins, "they are just the ordinary sort of Christian, like the rest of us, anxious to do the best they can for themselves, and not too particular as to doing other people in the process."

"I am inclined to think, Mrs. Wilkins," I said, "that you are not very far from the truth. A friend of mine, a year ago, was very bitter on this subject of Chinese cheap labour. A little later there died a distant relative of his who left him twenty thousand South African mining shares. He thinks now that to object to the Chinese is narrow-minded, illiberal, and against all religious teaching. He has bought an abridged edition of Confucius, and tells me that there is much that is ennobling in Chinese morality. Indeed, I gather from him that the introduction of the Chinese into South Africa will be the saving of that country. The noble Chinese will afford an object lesson to the poor white man, displaying to him the virtues of sobriety, thrift, and humility. I also gather that it will be of inestimable benefit to the noble Chinee himself. The Christian missionary will get hold of him in bulk, so to speak, and imbue him with the higher theology. It appears to be one of those rare cases where everybody is benefited at the expense of nobody. It is always a pity to let these rare opportunities slip by."

"Well," said Mrs. Wilkins, "I've nothin' to say agen the China-man, as a Chinaman. As to 'is being a 'eathen, well, throwin' stones at a church, as the sayin' is, don't make a Christian of you. There's Christians I've met as couldn't do themselves much 'arm by changing their religion; and as to cleanliness, well, I've never met but one, and 'e was a washerwoman, and I'd rather 'ave sat next to 'im in a third-class carriage on a Bank 'Oliday than next to some of 'em.

"Seems to me," continued Mrs. Wilkins, "we've got into the 'abit of talkin' a bit too much about other people's dirt. The London atmosphere ain't nat'rally a dry-cleanin' process in itself, but there's a goodish few as seem to think it is. One comes across Freeborn Britons 'ere and there as I'd be sorry to scrub clean for a shillin' and find my own soap."

"It is a universal failing, Mrs. Wilkins," I explained. "If you talk to a travelled Frenchman, he contrasts to his own satisfaction the Paris ouvrier in his blue blouse with the appearance of the London labourer."

"I daresay they're all right according to their lights," said Mrs. Wilkins, "but it does seem a bit wrong that if our own chaps are willin' and anxious to work, after all they've done, too, in the way of getting the mines for us, they shouldn't be allowed the job."

"Again, Mrs. Wilkins, it is difficult to arrive at a just conclusion," I said. "The mine-owner, according to his enemies, hates the British workman with the natural instinct that evil creatures feel towards the noble and virtuous. He will go to trouble and expense merely to spite the British workman, to keep him out of South Africa. According to his friends, the mine-owner sets his face against the idea of white labour for two reasons. First and foremost, it is not nice work; the mine-owner hates the thought of his beloved white brother toiling in the mines. It is not right that the noble white man should demean himself by such work. Secondly, white labour is too expensive. If for digging gold men had to be paid anything like the same prices they are paid for digging coal, the mines could not be worked. The world would lose the gold that the mine-owner is anxious to bestow upon it.

"The mine-owner, following his own inclinations, would take a little farm, grow potatoes, and live a beautiful life—perhaps write a little poetry. A slave to sense of duty, he is chained to the philanthropic work of gold-mining. If we hamper him and worry him the danger is that he will get angry with us—possibly he will order his fiery chariot and return to where he came from."

"Well, 'e can't take the gold with him, wherever 'e goes to?" argued Mrs. Wilkins.

"You talk, Mrs. Wilkins," I said, "as if the gold were of more value to the world than is the mine-owner."

"Well, isn't it?" demanded Mrs. Wilkins.

"It's a new idea, Mrs. Wilkins," I answered; "it wants thinking out."

HOW TO SOLVE THE SERVANT PROBLEM.

"*I am* glad to see, Mrs. Wilkins," I said, "that the Women's Domestic Guild of America has succeeded in solving the servant girl problem—none too soon, one might almost say."

"Ah," said Mrs. Wilkins, as she took the cover off the bacon and gave an extra polish to the mustard-pot with her apron, "they are clever people over there; leastways, so I've always 'eard."

"This, their latest, Mrs. Wilkins," I said, "I am inclined to regard as their greatest triumph. My hope is that the Women's Domestic Guild of America, when it has finished with the United States and Canada, will, perhaps, see its way to establishing a branch in England. There are ladies of my acquaintance who would welcome, I feel sure, any really satisfactory solution of the problem."

"Well, good luck to it, is all I say," responded Mrs. Wilkins, "and if it makes all the gals contented with their places, and all the mistresses satisfied with what they've got and 'appy in their minds, why, God bless it, say I."

"The mistake hitherto," I said, "from what I read, appears to have been that the right servant was not sent to the right place. What the Women's Domestic Guild of America proposes to do is to find the right servant for the right place. You see the difference, don't you, Mrs. Wilkins?"

"That's the secret," agreed Mrs. Wilkins. They don't anticipate any difficulty in getting the right sort of gal, I take it?"

"I gather not, Mrs. Wilkins," I replied.

Mrs. Wilkins is of a pessimistic turn of mind.

"I am not so sure about it," she said; "the Almighty don't seem to 'ave made too many of that sort. Unless these American ladies that you speak of are going to start a factory of their own. I am afraid there is disappointment in store for them."

"Don't throw cold water on the idea before it is fairly started, Mrs. Wilkins," I pleaded.

"Well, sir," said Mrs. Wilkins, "I 'ave been a gal myself in service; and in my time I've 'ad a few mistresses of my own, and I've 'eard a good deal about others. There are ladies and ladies, as you may know, sir, and some of them, if they aren't exactly angels, are about as near to it as can be looked for in this climate, and they are not the ones that do most of the complaining. But, as for the average mistress—well it ain't a gal she wants, it's a plaster image, without any natural innards—a sort of thing as ain't 'uman, and ain't to be found in 'uman nature. And then she'd grumble at it, if it didn't 'appen to be able to be in two places at once."

"You fear that the standard for that 'right girl' is likely to be set a trifle too high Mrs. Wilkins," I suggested.

"That 'right gal,' according to the notions of some of 'em," retorted Mrs. Wilkins, "'er place ain't down 'ere among us mere mortals; 'er place is up in 'eaven with a 'arp and a golden crown. There's my niece, Emma, I don't say she is a saint, but a better 'earted, 'arder working gal, at twenty pounds a year, you don't expect to find, unless maybe you're a natural born fool that can't 'elp yourself. She wanted a place. She 'ad been 'ome for nearly six months, nursing 'er old father, as 'ad been down all the winter with rheumatic fever; and 'ard-put to it she was for a few clothes. You 'ear 'em talk about gals as insists on an hour a day for practising the piano, and the right to invite their young man to spend the evening with them in the drawing-room. Perhaps it is meant to be funny; I ain't come across that type of gal myself, outside the pictures in the comic papers; and I'll never believe, till I see 'er myself, that anybody else 'as. They sent 'er from the registry office to a lady at Clapton.

"'I 'ope you are good at getting up early in the morning?' says the lady, 'I like a gal as rises cheerfully to 'er work.'

"'Well, ma'am,' says Emma, 'I can't say as I've got a passion for it. But it's one of those things that 'as to be done, and I guess I've learnt the trick.'

"'I'm a great believer in early rising,' says my lady; 'in the morning, one is always fresher for one's work; my 'usband and the younger children breakfast at 'arf past seven; myself and my eldest daughter 'ave our breakfest in bed at eight.'

'That'll be all right, ma'am,' says Emma.

"'And I 'ope,' says the lady, 'you are of an amiable disposition. Some gals when you ring the bell come up looking so disagreeable, one almost wishes one didn't want them.'

"'Well, it ain't a thing,' explains Emma, 'as makes you want to burst out laughing, 'earing the bell go off for the twentieth time, and 'aving suddenly to put down your work at, perhaps, a critical moment. Some ladies don't seem able to reach down their 'at for themselves.'

"'I 'ope you are not impertinent,' says the lady; 'if there's one thing that I object to in a servant it is impertinence.'

"'We none of us like being answered back,' says Emma, 'more particularly when we are in the wrong. But I know my place ma'am, and I shan't give you no lip. It always leads to less trouble, I find, keeping your mouth shut, rather than opening it.'

"'Are you fond of children,' asks my lady.

"'It depends upon the children,' says Emma; 'there are some I 'ave 'ad to do with as made the day seem pleasanter, and I've come across others as I could 'ave parted from at any moment without tears.'

"'I like a gal,' says the lady, 'who is naturally fond of children, it shows a good character.'

"'How many of them are there?' says Emma.

"'Four of them,' answers my lady, 'but you won't 'ave much to do except with the two youngest. The great thing with young children is to surround them with good examples. Are you a Christian?' asks my lady.

"'That's what I'm generally called,' says Emma.

"'Every other Sunday evening out is my rule,' says the lady, 'but of course I shall expect you to go to church.'

"'Do you mean in my time, ma'am,' says Emma, 'or in yours.'

"'I mean on your evening of course,' says my lady. ''Ow else could you go?'

"'Well, ma'am,' says Emma, 'I like to see my people now and then.'

"'There are better things,' says my lady, 'than seeing what you call your people, and I should not care to take a girl into my 'ouse as put 'er pleasure before 'er religion. You are not engaged, I 'ope?'

"'Walking out, ma'am, do you mean?' says Emma. 'No, ma'am, there is nobody I've got in my mind—not just at present.'

"'I never will take a gal,' explains my lady, 'who is engaged. I find it distracts 'er attention from 'er work. And I must insist if you come to me,' continues my lady, 'that you get yourself another 'at and jacket. If there is one thing I object to in a servant it is a disposition to cheap finery.'

"'Er own daughter was sitting there beside 'er with 'alf a dozen silver bangles on 'er wrist, and a sort of thing 'anging around 'er neck, as, 'ad it been real, would 'ave been worth perhaps a thousand pounds. But Emma wanted a job, so she kept 'er thoughts to 'erself.

"'I can put these things by and get myself something else,' she says, 'if you don't mind, ma'am, advancing me something out of my first three months' wages. I'm afraid my account at the bank is a bit overdrawn.'

"The lady whispered something to 'er daughter. 'I am afraid, on thinking it over,' she says, 'that you won't suit, after all. You don't look serious enough. I feel sure, from the way you do your 'air,' says my lady, 'there's a frivolous side to your nature.'

"So Emma came away, and was not, on the whole, too sorry."

"But do they get servants to come to them, this type of mistress, do you think, Mrs. Wilkins?" I asked.

"They get them all right," said Mrs. Wilkins, "and if it's a decent gal, it makes a bad gal of 'er, that ever afterwards looks upon every mistress as 'er enemy, and acts accordingly. And if she ain't a naturally good gal, it makes 'er worse, and then you 'ear what awful things gals are. I don't say it's an easy problem," continued Mrs. Wilkins, "it's just like marriages. The good mistress gets 'old of the bad servant, and the bad mistress, as often as not is lucky."

"But how is it," I argued, "that in hotels, for instance, the service is excellent, and the girls, generally speaking, seem contented? The work is hard, and the wages not much better, if as good."

"Ah," said Mrs. Wilkins, "you 'ave 'it the right nail on the 'ead, there, sir. They go into the 'otels and work like niggers, knowing that if a single thing goes wrong they will be bully-ragged and sworn at till they don't know whether they are standing on their 'ead or their 'eels. But they 'ave their hours; the gal knows when 'er work is done, and when the clock strikes she is a 'uman being once again. She 'as got that moment to look forward to all day, and it keeps 'er going. In private service there's no moment in the day to 'ope for. If the lady is reasonable she ain't overworked; but no 'ow can she ever feel she is her own mistress, free to come and go, to wear 'er bit of finery, to 'ave 'er bit of fun. She works from six in the morning till eleven or twelve at night, and then she only goes to bed provided she ain't wanted. She don't belong to 'erself at all; it's that that irritates them."

"I see your point, Mrs. Wilkins," I said, "and, of course, in a house where two or three servants were kept some such plan might easily be arranged. The girl who commenced work at six o'clock in the morning might consider herself free at six o'clock in the evening. What she did with herself, how she dressed herself in her own time, would be her affair. What church the clerk or the workman belongs to, what company he keeps, is no concern of the firm. In such matters, mistresses, I am inclined to think, saddle themselves with a responsibility for which there is no need. If the girl behaves herself while in the house, and does her work, there the contract ends. The mistress who thinks it her duty to combine the roles of employer and of maiden aunt is naturally resented. The next month the girl might change her hours from twelve to twelve, and her fellow-servant could enjoy the six a.m. to six p.m. shift. But how do you propose to deal, Mrs. Wilkins, with the smaller menage, that employs only one servant?"

"Well, sir," said Mrs. Wilkins, "it seems to me simple enough. Ladies talk pretty about the dignity of labour, and are never tired of pointing out why gals should prefer domestic service to all other kinds of work. Suppose they practise what they preach. In the 'ouse, where there's only the master and the mistress, and, say a couple of small children, let the lady take her turn. After all, it's only her duty, same as the office or the shop is the man's. Where, on the other 'and, there are biggish boys and gals about the place, well it wouldn't do them any 'arm to be taught to play a little less, and to look after themselves a little more. It's just arranging things—that's all that's wanted."

"You remind me of a family I once knew, Mrs. Wilkins," I said; "it consisted of the usual father and mother, and of five sad, healthy girls. They kept two servants—or, rather, they never kept any servants; they lived always looking for servants, breaking their hearts over servants, packing servants off at a moment's notice, standing disconsolately looking after servants who had packed themselves off at a moment's notice, wondering generally what the world was coming too. It occurred to me at the time, that without much trouble, they could have lived a peaceful life without servants. The eldest girl was learning painting—and seemed unable to learn anything else. It was poor sort of painting; she noticed it herself. But she seemed to think that, if she talked a lot about it, and thought of nothing else, that somehow it would all come right. The second girl played the violin. She played it from early morning till late evening, and friends fell away from them. There wasn't a spark of talent in the family, but they all had a notion that a vague longing to be admired was just the same as genius.

"Another daughter fancied she would like to be an actress, and screamed all day in the attic. The fourth wrote poetry on a typewriter, and wondered why nobody seemed to want it; while the fifth one suffered from a weird belief that smearing wood with a red-hot sort of poker was a thing worth doing for its own sake. All of them seemed willing enough to work, provided only that it was work of no use to any living soul. With a little sense, and the occasional assistance of a char-woman, they could have led a merrier life."

"If I was giving away secrets," said Mrs. Wilkins, "I'd say to the mistresses: 'Show yourselves able to be independent.' It's because the gals know that the mistresses can't do without them that they sometimes gives themselves airs."

WHY WE HATE THE FOREIGNER.

The advantage that the foreigner possesses over the Englishman is that he is born good. He does not have to try to be good, as we do. He does not have to start the New Year with the resolution to be good, and succeed, bar accidents, in being so till the middle of January. He is just good all the year round. When a foreigner is told to mount or descend from a tram on the near side, it does not occur to him that it would be humanly possible to secure egress from or ingress to that tram from the off side.

In Brussels once I witnessed a daring attempt by a lawless foreigner to enter a tram from the wrong side. The gate was open: he was standing close beside it. A line of traffic was in his way: to have got round to the right side of that tram would have meant missing it. He entered when the conductor was not looking, and took his seat. The astonishment of the conductor on finding him there was immense. How did he get there? The conductor had been watching the proper entrance, and the man had not passed him. Later, the true explanation suggested itself to the conductor, but for a while he hesitated to accuse a fellow human being of such crime.

He appealed to the passenger himself. Was his presence to be accounted for by miracle or by sin? The passenger confessed. It was more in sorrow than in anger that the conductor requested him at once to leave. This tram was going to be kept respectable. The passenger proved refractory, a halt was called, and the gendarmerie appealed to. After the manner of policemen, they sprang, as it were, from the ground, and formed up behind an imposing officer, whom I took to be the sergeant. At first the sergeant could hardly believe the conductor's statement. Even then, had the passenger asserted that he had entered by the proper entrance, his word would have been taken. Much easier to the foreign official mind would it have been to believe that the conductor had been stricken with temporary blindness, than that man born of woman would have deliberately done anything expressly forbidden by a printed notice.

Myself, in his case, I should have lied and got the trouble over. But he was a proud man, or had not much sense—one of the two, and so held fast to the truth. It was pointed out to him that he must descend immediately and wait for the next tram. Other gendarmes were arriving from every quarter: resistance in the circumstances seemed hopeless. He said he would get down. He made to descend this time by the proper gate, but that was not justice. He had mounted the wrong side, he must alight on the wrong side. Accordingly, he was put out amongst the traffic, after which the conductor preached a sermon from the centre of the tram on the danger of ascents and descents conducted from the wrong quarter.

There is a law throughout Germany—an excellent law it is: I would we had it in England—that nobody may scatter paper about the street. An English military friend told me that, one day in Dresden, unacquainted with this rule, he tore a long letter he had been reading into some fifty fragments and threw them behind him. A policeman stopped him and explained to him quite politely the law upon the subject. My military friend agreed that it was a very good law, thanked the man for his information, and said that for the future he would bear it in mind. That, as the policeman pointed out, would make things right enough for the future, but meanwhile it was necessary to deal with the past—with the fifty or so pieces of paper lying scattered about the road and pavement.

My military friend, with a pleasant laugh, confessed he did not see what was to be done. The policeman, more imaginative, saw a way out. It was that my military friend should set to work and pick up those fifty scraps of paper. He is an English General on the Retired List, and of imposing appearance: his manner on occasion is haughty. He did not see himself on his hands and knees in the chief street of Dresden, in the middle of the afternoon, picking up paper.

The German policeman himself admitted that the situation was awkward. If the English General could not accept it there happened to be an alternative. It was that the English General should accompany the policeman through the streets, followed by the usual crowd, to the nearest prison, some three miles off. It being now four o'clock in the afternoon, they would probably find the judge departed. But the most comfortable thing possible in prison cells should be allotted to him, and the policeman had little doubt that the General, having paid his fine of forty marks, would find himself a free man again in time for lunch the following day. The general suggested hiring a boy to pick up the paper.

The policeman referred to the wording of the law, and found that this would not be permitted.

"I thought the matter out," my friend told me, "imagining all the possible alternatives, including that of knocking the fellow down and making a bolt, and came to the conclusion that his first suggestion would, on the whole, result in the least discomfort. But I had no idea that picking up small scraps of thin paper off greasy stones was the business that I found it! It took me nearly ten minutes, and afforded amusement, I calculate, to over a thousand people. But it is a good law, mind you: all I wish is that I had known it beforehand."

On one occasion I accompanied an American lady to a German Opera House. The taking-off of hats in the German Schausspielhaus is obligatory, and again I would it were so in England. But the American lady is accustomed to disregard rules made by mere man. She explained to the doorkeeper that she was going to wear her hat. He, on his side, explained to her that she was not: they were both a bit short with one another. I took the opportunity to turn aside and buy a programme: the fewer people there are mixed up in an argument, I always think, the better.

My companion explained quite frankly to the doorkeeper that it did not matter what he said, she was not going to take any notice of him. He did not look a talkative man at any time, and, maybe, this announcement further discouraged him. In any case, he made no attempt to answer. All he did was to stand in the centre of the doorway with a far-away look in his eyes. The doorway was some four feet wide: he was about three feet six across, and weighed about twenty stone. As I explained, I was busy buying a programme, and when I returned my friend had her hat in her hand, and was digging pins into it: I think she was trying to make believe it was the heart of the doorkeeper. She did not want to listen to the opera, she wanted to talk all the time about that doorkeeper, but the people round us would not even let her do that.

She has spent three winters in Germany since then. Now when she feels like passing through a door that is standing wide open just in front of her, and which leads to just the place she wants to get to, and an official shakes his head at her, and explains that she must not, but must go up two flights of stairs and along a corridor and down another flight of stairs, and so get to her place that way, she apologises for her error and trots off looking ashamed of herself.

Continental Governments have trained their citizens to perfection. Obedience is the Continent's first law. The story that is told of a Spanish king who was nearly drowned because the particular official whose duty it was to dive in after Spanish kings when they tumbled out of boats happened to be dead, and his successor had not yet been appointed, I can quite believe. On the Continental railways if you ride second class with a first-class ticket you render yourself liable to imprisonment. What the penalty is for riding first with a second-class ticket I cannot say—probably death, though a friend of mine came very near on one occasion to finding out.

All would have gone well with him if he had not been so darned honest. He is one of those men who pride themselves on being honest. I believe he takes a positive pleasure in being honest. He had purchased a second-class ticket for a station up a mountain, but meeting, by chance on the platform, a lady acquaintance, had gone with her into a first-class apartment. On arriving at the journey's end he explained to the collector what he had done, and, with his purse in his hand, demanded to know the difference. They took him into a room and locked the door. They wrote out his confession and read it over to him, and made him sign it, and then they sent for a policeman.

The policeman cross-examined him for about a quarter of an hour. They did not believe the story about the lady. Where was the lady? He did not know. They searched the neighbourhood for her, but could not find her. He suggested—what turned out to be the truth—that, tired of loitering about the station, she had gone up the mountain. An Anarchist outrage had occurred in the neighbouring town some months before. The policeman suggested searching for bombs. Fortunately, a Cook's agent, returning with a party of tourists, arrived upon the scene, and took it upon himself to explain in delicate language that my friend was a bit of an ass and could not tell first class from second. It was the red cushions that had deceived my friend: he thought it was first class, as a matter of fact it was second class.

Everybody breathed again. The confession was torn up amid universal joy: and then the fool of a ticket collector wanted to know about the lady—who must have travelled in a second-class compartment with a first-class ticket. It looked as if a bad time were in store for her on her return to the station.

But the admirable representative of Cook was again equal to the occasion. He explained that my friend was also a bit of a liar. When he said he had travelled with this lady he was merely boasting. He would like to have travelled with her, that was all he meant, only his German was shaky. Joy once more entered upon the scene. My friend's character appeared to be re-established. He was not the abandoned wretch for whom they had taken him—only, apparently, a wandering idiot. Such an one the German official could respect. At the expense of such an one the German official even consented to drink beer.

Not only the foreign man, woman and child, but the foreign dog is born good. In England, if you happen to be the possessor of a dog, much of your time is taken up dragging him out of fights, quarrelling with the possessor of the other dog as to which began it, explaining to irate elderly ladies that he did not kill the cat, that the cat must have died of heart disease while running across the road, assuring disbelieving game-keepers that he is not your dog, that you have not the faintest notion whose dog he is. With the foreign dog, life is a peaceful proceeding. When the foreign dog sees a row, tears spring to his eyes: he hastens on and tries to find a policeman. When the foreign dog sees a cat in a hurry, he stands aside to allow her to pass. They dress the foreign dog—some of them—in a little coat, with a pocket for his handkerchief, and put shoes on his feet. They have not given him a hat—not yet. When they do, he will contrive by some means or another to raise it politely when he meets a cat he thinks he knows.

One morning, in a Continental city, I came across a disturbance—it might be more correct to say the disturbance came across me: it swept down upon me, enveloped me before I knew that I was in it. A fox-terrier it was, belonging to a very young lady—it was when the disturbance was to a certain extent over that we discovered he belonged to this young lady. She arrived towards the end of the disturbance, very much out of breath: she had been running for a mile, poor girl, and shouting most of the way. When she looked round and saw all the things that had happened, and had had other things that she had missed explained to her, she burst into tears. An English owner of that fox-terrier would have given one look round and then have jumped upon the nearest tram going anywhere. But, as I have said, the foreigner is born good. I left her giving her name and address to seven different people.

But it was about the dog I wished to speak more particularly. He had commenced innocently enough, trying to catch a sparrow. Nothing delights a sparrow more than being chased by a dog. A dozen times he thought he had the sparrow. Then another dog had got in his way. I don't know what they call this breed of dog, but abroad it is popular: it has no tail and looks like a pig—when things are going well with it. This particular specimen, when I saw him, looked more like part of a doormat. The fox-terrier had seized it by the scruff of the neck and had rolled it over into the gutter just in front of a motor cycle. Its owner, a large lady, had darted out to save it, and had collided with the motor cyclist. The large lady had been thrown some half a dozen yards against an Italian boy carrying a tray load of plaster images.

I have seen a good deal of trouble in my life, but never one yet that did not have an Italian image-vendor somehow or other mixed up in it. Where these boys hide in times of peace is a mystery. The chance of being upset brings them out as sunshine brings out flies. The motor cycle had dashed into a little milk-cart and had spread it out neatly in the middle of the tram lines. The tram traffic looked like being stopped for a quarter of an hour; but the idea of every approaching tram driver appeared to be that if he rang his bell with sufficient vigor this seeming obstruction would fade away and disappear.

In an English town all this would not have attracted much attention. Somebody would have explained that a dog was the original cause, and the whole series of events would have appeared ordinary and natural. Upon these foreigners the fear descended that the Almighty, for some reason, was angry with them. A policeman ran to catch the dog.

The delighted dog rushed backwards, barking furiously, and tried to throw up paving stones with its hind legs. That frightened a nursemaid who was wheeling a perambulator, and then it was that I entered into the proceedings. Seated on the edge of the pavement, with a perambulator on one side of me and a howling baby on the other, I told that dog what I thought of him.

Forgetful that I was in a foreign land—that he might not understand me—I told it him in English, I told it him at length, I told it very loud and clear. He stood a yard in front of me, listening to me with an expression of ecstatic joy I have never before or since seen equalled on any face, human or canine. He drank it in as though it had been music from Paradise.

"Where have I heard that song before?" he seemed to be saying to himself, "the old familiar language they used to talk to me when I was young?"

He approached nearer to me; there were almost tears in his eyes when I had finished.

"Say it again!" he seemed to be asking of me. "Oh! say it all over again, the dear old English oaths and curses that in this God-forsaken land I never hoped to hear again."

I learnt from the young lady that he was an English-born fox-terrier. That explained everything. The foreign dog does not do this sort of thing. The foreigner is born good: that is why we hate him.

www.ingramcontent.com/pod-product-compliance
Lightning Source LLC
Chambersburg PA
CBHW020250150626
46552CB00020B/753